everyday ayurveda cooking
for a calm, clear mind

Also by Kate O'Donnell

The Everyday Ayurveda Cookbook: A Seasonal Guide to Eating and Living Well

The Everyday Ayurveda Guide to Self-Care: Rhythms, Routines, and Home Remedies for Natural Healing

everyday ayurveda cooking
for a calm, clear mind

100 SIMPLE SATTVIC RECIPES

—————

KATE O'DONNELL

PHOTOGRAPHS BY CARA BROSTROM

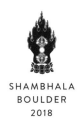

SHAMBHALA
BOULDER
2018

Shambhala Publications, Inc.
2129 13th Street
Boulder, Colorado 80302
www.shambhala.com

9 8 7 6 5

Printed in the United States of America

♾ This edition is printed on acid-free paper that meets the
American National Standards Institute Z39.48 Standard.
♻ Shambhala Publications makes every effort to print on recycled paper.
For more information please visit www.shambhala.com.

Shambhala Publications is distributed worldwide by
Penguin Random House, Inc., and its subsidiaries.

Designed by Allison Meierding

Library of Congress Cataloging-in-Publication Data

Names: O'Donnell, Kate (Ayurvedic practitioner) author.
Title: Everyday Ayurveda cooking for a calm, clear mind: 100 simple sattvic
recipes/Kate O'Donnell; photography by Cara Brostrom.
Description: First edition. | Boulder: Shambhala, [2018] | Includes index.
Identifiers: LCCN 2017011440 | ISBN 9781611804478 (pbk.: alk. paper)
Subjects: LCSH: Medicine, Ayurvedic. | Mind and body. | LCGFT: Cookbooks.
Classification: LCC R605 .O32 2018 | DDC 615.5/38—dc23
LC record available at https://lccn.loc.gov/2017011440

This book is dedicated to the Ayur Vidya, the spirit of Ayurveda,
and to all the gurus and vaidyas of past, present, and future.

CONTENTS

INTRODUCTION TO
EVERYDAY AYURVEDA COOKING FOR A CALM, CLEAR MIND

———

HALFWAY THROUGH WRITING the *Everyday Ayurveda Cookbook*, I knew I had to write a cookbook about the *sattvic* diet, the aspect of Ayurveda that focuses on life-giving, pure foods to promote harmony in the mind. While writing about the Ayurvedic diet and lifestyle, I kept coming back to how important mental balance is in becoming aware of our bodies, our food choices, and how we care for ourselves. Understanding our bodies' natural rhythms and how to listen to the signs our bodies give us are the key to self-empowered health. Yet what has intrigued me most in my Ayurvedic practice is the role that the mind plays in our ability to listen, heal, and maintain a healthy lifestyle. I started to think how wonderful it would be to write *another* cookbook—one that could help readers access the benefits of food for their moods and overall mental balance.

The connection between stress and modern ailments is becoming clearer through scientific research—reinforcing the importance of a body/mind connection that has always been at the heart of Ayurveda. The more people I work with—observing this science as it applies to the matrix of household living and the balance of work, family, self-care, and self-evolution—the more I see the importance of mental balance in maintaining health and happiness.

Have you noticed that certain foods can settle you down or pick you up? Ayurveda helps us understand how foods affect our mental wellness by balancing certain energies—specifically, satisfaction, passion, or lassitude. The sattvic diet is a way of eating to keep a simple, contented mental energy alive, and it involves eating more fresh, local foods; being thoughtful about how we prepare them; and sitting down to enjoy them. For me, this way of eating has come naturally as a companion to my yoga practice, and I believe it was this synergy of yoga and Ayurveda that drew me to the diet in the first place. Paying attention to how food makes me feel, not just in my gut, but in both my mood and my heart, has led to a healthy body and a happy head. A former extremist, I've learned about balance by experimenting with all manner of fad diets over the years. I've tried it all, which may make me the ideal guide. It's been a process and not always an easy one. Throughout this book, I will share my story with you and give you some practical tips to help you make the sattvic diet part of your life.

Cara Brostrom, the photographer and recipe developer, had her second baby while we were creating this book together. I asked her for her first impressions as I was writing, and she said, "Sure, I want to do all these things you're talking about, but can you write to those of us who are being pulled in many directions?" I started to think about the fact that many of us do not have a lot of free time and brain space in the day to learn new routines. We *are* pulled in so many directions in our lives—by the media, family, the beliefs we have about work and play. How do we attend to our mental state in the middle of it all? In this book, I draw from my own experiences of trial and error, share my pitfalls and successes with you, and help to translate an ancient roadmap for balanced living. This book is for *you*, the busy, heartfelt, and sometimes overwhelmed reader. Eating a sattvic diet helps me notice how my choices are affecting me and offers delicious alternatives that help me with energy and calm. I am inspired to share this knowledge and some of the easy recipes I've invented along the way because, as I teach others, I keep seeing that Ayurveda really works.

While Ayurveda is an epic, sophisticated, time-honored system of medicine, I'm pointing out some of the sattvic diet and lifestyle practices that fit our modern life-style. Everything you see in this book, from the food to the photo shoots, is grassroots and a product of my supportive community. If we can do it, you can do it too. *Sattva*, the clear essence of mind, boils down to simplicity and beauty. Through these simple recipes and Cara's beautiful photographs of real food and real people in real places, I hope to inspire you to cultivate satisfaction and peace of mind every day.

about *everyday ayurveda cooking for a calm, clear mind*

The sattvic diet fosters balance, whether you completely understand the system or not. But I've noticed people are more likely to practice it if they feel they under-stand it. It is not a quick fix, but the lifestyle changes will happen gradually if you are patient.

"Slowly and slowly," as my yoga teacher always said. So, while you don't have to read and digest all the information in Part One of this book to benefit from the recipes and practice tips, a little background may inspire action. In my first book, *The Everyday Ayurveda Cookbook*, I explored the foundations of Ayurveda and gave a thorough overview of this ancient health system and how it works. For those of you who read my first book, some of the information in chapter 1 will be familiar, but it is worth re-reading to refresh your understanding of Ayurvedic basics. After the introductory chapter, you will be in new territory—understanding the mental energetics of food and how they affect your mood.

We will journey into the mind from the Ayurvedic point of view. To find balance, we have to know the mind as an instrument of the intuitive self rather than letting it run the show. We'll be taking a step back to observe mental processes and how the mind works. Once you have this new awareness of your mind and how it can better serve you, it will be easier to choose healthy food and navigate the day with clarity.

The key is understanding that certain foods support a clear mind, while others can amp things up or cloud things over. Getting to know the energies of your mind will take some time, and this book is full of suggestions to help you explore how your diet and lifestyle can be tools for mental wellness. Time and time again, I have seen people begin with this type of cooking to feel more centered, and from there, they start to look at their mental and emotional states. This is why I focus on a food-based program for bringing the mind back into balance. Food can be delicious, medicinal, and spiritual.

To help you on your way, Part Two includes three recipe sections: foods that cultivate contentment, those that calm the mind, and those that vitalize and motivate. You can cook freely from the entire book and promote sattva, but to further refine the concept, you can try using the different sections to address shifts in mental energy. Or you may just like to cook whatever looks most delicious. The bonus is that the act of cooking itself promotes healing.

While I've learned a lot about sattvic cooking in India, I still live in the West, so I have provided a blend of traditional recipes like dal and *dosa* with spins on familiar dishes like Sattvic Noodle Bowl and Peach Blueberry Cobbler. You will see that the sattvic diet is a vegetarian one, and I will explore some of the ways this tradition preserves vitality through healthy fats, as well as nourishing legume and grain combinations. I will help you make a gentle transition to sattvic eating with some of my trademark hybridized recipes like smoothies, quick pickles, and variations on traditional *kichari*. It's a diverse, exciting selection of delicious recipes that will help you feel wonderful from the inside out!

PART ONE

AYURVEDA AND THE BODY/MIND CONNECTION

1

a
brief introduction
to ayurveda

WHILE AYURVEDA, India's indigenous health system, is a vast and ancient subject, much of its common-sense wisdom is applicable today. My favorite thing about Ayurveda is the central role that food plays in well-being. Whether you like to cook or not, food is medicine for the mind, and a little intention in your diet can truly change your perspective on life. Harmonizing the energies of the mind can relieve stress, increase joy, and foster spiritual connection. What's not to love?

To ensure success, we'll be keeping our discussion simple in both theory and practice. You don't have to read this book cover to cover to benefit from the recipes, but it never hurts to have a clear road map for the journey. This brief introduction will set the stage for our exploration of the mind, how food affects the mind, and how you can apply Ayurveda in your own life to create mental balance.

the origins of ayurveda

Ayurveda (pronounced "EYE-yer-VAY-da") may be the oldest continually practiced health system in the world, dating from two thousand to five thousand years ago. The earliest information on Ayurveda is contained in the *Rig Veda*, one of four bodies of ancient scripture that were orally transmitted in lyrical phrases called *sutras* (threads). The Vedas are believed to originate from the *rishis*, sages in deep states of meditation.

Ayurveda can be loosely translated as the "science of life." The classical text the Charaka Samhita describes *Ayur*, or "life," as being made up of four parts: the physical body, the mind, the soul, and the senses (sight, hearing, touch, smell, and taste). Contrary to Western models, which have traditionally focused mostly on the physical body, Ayurveda has always given attention to the health of all four of the fundamental aspects of life. The system looks at the whole person—using diet, biorhythms, herbal medicine, psychology, wholesome lifestyle, surgery, and therapeutic bodywork to address the root cause of disease. Ayurvedic hospitals and clinics abound in India, where Western medicine is often used in conjunction with the traditional methods. Whereas Western medicine excels at resolving acute situations, Ayurveda stands out as a preventive medicine—seeking to halt the progression from imbalance to disease by addressing the underlying causes early on.

Thousands of Years of Trial and Error

— ◆ ◆ ◆ —

I will occasionally quote from classic texts to remind us that this information comes from thousands of years ago and was collected over millennia by both scientists and sages. Most commonly, I use the Charaka Samhita, a seven-volume set that describes pathology and treatment for thousands of ailments, as well as a philosophical background for Ayurveda. Information on the texts quoted—the Charaka Samhita, the Ashtanga Hrdayam (a compilation of teachings from the Charaka and Sushruta Samhitas), and the Bhagavad Gita—can be found in the resource section at the back of this book.

THE BIG PICTURE

Ayurveda recognizes that every human being is a microcosm (a small part or reflection) of the macrocosm (the big picture or universe). Our minds and bodies are made up of the same elements that make up everything around us, and we are moved by the same energies or forces that move the oceans, the winds, the stars, and the planets.

The philosophy behind Ayurveda is simple: just as the cycles of the sun, moon, tides, and seasons ebb and flow, so do we. The introduction of artificial light, global food transportation, and a busy schedule make it easy to get out of sync with nature's rhythms.

Ayurveda and Yoga actually stem from the same philosophical roots and have a shared goal of creating a union between microcosm and macrocosm. Yoga is a pathway for navigating the connection of the mind and body with the larger world around us. The sattvic diet, sometimes called the yogic diet, is a part of this path. In these modern times, when many suffer in body and mind due to a lack of connection, the shared goal of Yoga and Ayurveda to unite mind, body, and spirit couldn't come at a better time. Ayurveda often uses the movements and breathing techniques from yoga to access the energy body, promoting the smooth circulation of energy throughout the body and mind, which is especially helpful for managing stress and restoring the body's natural rhythms.

If you get out of sync with natural rhythms—for example, by eating tropical fruits in winter or processed foods, staying up all night, or working all day without a break—your body and mind will become out of whack. The link between the mind and overall health is clear—imbalance in one will lead to imbalance in the other. Like a fish swimming upstream, going against natural currents will slow you down. Inevitably, you will start to feel tired, anxious, or depressed, and over time, you will end up "out of order."

THE POWER OF DIGESTION

Healthy digestion is the most fundamental aspect of overall wellness in Ayurveda. The complete digestion, absorption, and assimilation of food nutrients create the building blocks of the body, called *ahara rasa*, or "the essence of food." When you chew and swallow your food, it mixes with water, enzymes, and acids, and the end product is the essence or juice, which is used to make tissues. In this way, healthy digestion makes a healthy body. Digesting food properly connects us to the essence of the food we eat every day and to our planet that provides this food. This explains why diet is a profound aspect of Ayurvedic healing.

Complete wellness, however, takes into account not only physical digestion in the stomach, but mental digestion as well. *The digestion of ideas, experiences, and emotions is a key function required for our overall well-being.* The right amount of input and enough space to process it result in a calm, steady mind and nervous system. This sustainable, low-stress reality underlies the health of the physical body as well.

The body and mind are interdependent systems affected by parallel influences: the physical world of the five elements, and the energetic world of stillness, movement, and change. It can be easier to recognize tangible elements in the body first, so let's look at body basics before we dive into the topic of mind.

the five elements

In Ayurveda, human anatomy starts with the five elements—ether (space), air, fire, water, and earth. The elements create three compounds that govern specific functions and energies in the body, namely, movement, transformation, and cohesion (holding things together). According to Charaka, when these compounds, known as *doshas*, are in balance and working harmoniously, you will enjoy smooth-moving processes (digestion, circulation, and so on), clear senses, the proper elimination of wastes, and happiness.

Each of these five elements manifests as qualities in the body that can be recognized simply by paying close attention to physical sensations. For example, air and space are cold and light, fire is hot and sharp, and earth and water are heavy and moist. Imbalance is brought on by too much or too little of any of these qualities. Too much dryness, say from living in the desert and eating dry crackers, will result in a symptom like dry skin. These elements can have corresponding effects on the mind, such as the heavy, moist qualities of earth and water resulting in brain fog, or the light, mobile qualities of air and space inhibiting focus. *Ayurveda manages these imbalances by introducing opposite qualities and reducing similar qualities.* For example, in the case of brain fog, introducing light, dry foods like barley and reducing heavy, moist foods like wheat will begin to alleviate the symptom.

Everyone requires all five elements, but they occur in different amounts in different bodies. Understanding your individual elemental makeup can take some time. By paying attention to your body over the course of changing seasons, you'll begin to recognize the major players. If dry skin, scalp, stool, and so on are a part of your world, it's likely there's a good deal of space and air elements in your body. Once this becomes clear, start feeling for the subtle qualities of these elements in your mind and moods. Space and air, for example, can manifest as an anxious, sometimes spacey, ungrounded, or sensitive mind or mood due to the porous nature of these elements.

Here's where you will find the five elements (*Pancha Mahabhutas*) in your body.

Space: Intestines, ears, center of the bones

Air: Anywhere there is movement, including belching, gas, and cracking joints

Fire: Stomach acid, bile, enzymes in the small intestine, red blood cells, metabolic processes

Water: Mucous membranes, lymphatic fluid, digestive juices, saliva, synovial fluid

Earth: Fat, muscle, bone

While it is important to understand how Ayurveda views the physical body, in this book we will be looking mostly at the mind. Ayurveda considers the functions of body and mind to be so interconnected that balance and imbalance are rooted in both physical and mental spheres. It is important to our overall well-being to understand both.

what is a dosha?

You have probably heard of the doshas. According to the Ashtanga Hrdayam, *dosha* literally means "that which is faulty." But doshas aren't a problem until imbalance has been hanging around awhile. These energies, each a synergy of two elements, can hurt or help you, depending on whether or not they are in a relative state of balance. That's why it is more important to understand how to maintain balance than it is to dwell on doshas as the "bad guys."

There are three doshas, known as *vata*, *pitta*, and *kapha*. These are the compounds that arise naturally when the five elements come together in the human body. Each performs a specific function in the body and manifests as a recognizable group of qualities. While the primary energies that affect the mind are different from the three doshas, when one or more of the doshas accumulate in your body, you are likely to notice the same qualities in your mind.

> **Vata** ("VA-tah") is the energy of movement.
> **Pitta** ("PITT-ah") is the energy of transformation.
> **Kapha** ("CUP-hah") is the energy of structure and lubrication together; cohesion (think glue).

VATA

Where there is space, air begins to move, and together these elements manifest as *cold, light, dry, rough, mobile, erratic,* and *clear* qualities. Think of vata as the currents of the body. The body knows the food goes in the mouth, then down and out; vata ushers it along. Vata also moves the attention and is responsible for the movements of the five senses and the activity of the brain and nervous system. The expansive nature of its qualities makes for a creative, mobile energy. There is nothing problematic about the qualities of space and air, or their function, unless your body has accumulated too much. Too many vata qualities can result in signs of imbalance such as gas and constipation, increasingly dry skin, and racing thoughts and anxiety.

Balanced Vata	Vata Imbalance
• Consistent elimination	• Gas and constipation
• Free breathing	• Asthma
• Good circulation	• Cold hands and feet
• Keen senses	• Anxiety/feeling overwhelmed
• Creativity	

PITTA

Where there is fire, there has to be water to keep it from burning everything up. The resulting compound is firewater, a *liquid, hot, sharp, penetrating, light, mobile, oily, smelly* grouping of qualities. (Think acid or bile.) When food gets chewed, pitta moves in to break it down, liquidize it, metabolize it, and transform it into tissues. It does the same with raw information, breaking it down, understanding it, and organizing it. The sharp, motivated nature of pitta makes for quick, focused energy. This is great, unless things get too hot or too sharp, resulting in signs of imbalance such as acidy burps or reflux; diarrhea; skin rashes; inflammation; or mental states that include irritability, obsession, and jealousy.

Pitta in Balance	Pitta Imbalance
• Good appetite and metabolism	• Acid indigestion, reflux
• Steady hormones	• Painful, heavy menstrual cycle
• Sharp eyesight	• Red, dry eyes; the need for glasses
• Comprehension	• Acne, rosacea
• Good complexion (rosy skin)	• Irritability
	• Tendency to overwork
	• Overly competitive

KAPHA

Without water, you wouldn't be able to get sand to stick together to build a sandcastle. The earth element requires water in this same way to get things to stick together. Kapha is like glue: *cool, liquid, slimy, heavy, slow, dull, dense,* and *stable.*

This group of qualities provides density in the bones and fat, cohesion in the tissues and joints, and plenty of mucus so we don't dry out. Its gentle, soft, sticky nature makes for a mellow, sweet energy and a strong memory. Great! Unless things get too heavy and too sticky, which can result in signs of imbalance such as loss of appetite; slow digestion; sinus troubles and allergies; weight gain; or mental states like heaviness, brain fog, and sadness.

Kapha in Balance	Kapha Imbalance
Strong bodily tissues	Excessive weight gain
Well-lubricated joints and mucous membranes	Water retention
Hearty immune system	Sinus or lung congestion
	Sadness, heavy heart

In an ideal world, we would all have a decent dose of all of these qualities and a balanced, well-functioning system. One person may be more fiery and prone to arguments, another may be more spacey and prone to forget things—that's the fun of variation in nature. The body's constitution, or makeup of the elements, is genetic. Understanding your constitution can help you understand which of these compounds is likely to get out of balance so you can make choices in your diet and lifestyle to keep potential doshas in check.

It's easy to focus on dosha, that which gets out of balance. But categorizing yourself as a dosha ("I'm so vata") or identifying yourself with states of imbalance is not the aim of Ayurvedic wisdom. It may be more helpful to understand and manage the general causes of imbalance first. For instance, if you notice you often feel overheated and irritable, and your imbalances tend toward characteristics on the pitta list, practice eating calming foods and making time to relax.

While the physical activity of the doshas certainly affects our mental state, Ayurveda is specific about subtle, energetic tools for understanding balance in the mind. There are three energies: *sattva* (the clear essence of the mind) and the two energies that act on it, *rajas* (restlessness) and *tamas* (stagnation). The Charaka Samhita considers rajas and tamas to be "doshas of the mind." The three mental energies can be balanced in the same way vata, pitta, and kapha are—by noticing imbalances early on. We will be learning about what these energies are and how they affect the mind and mood in the next chapter.

Ayurveda is a lifelong exploration and a path to self-realization. Please keep in mind that this chapter is a very basic introduction to these ideas, which have layers of meaning. I wanted to give you just enough information so that we have a simple, common language to illuminate the body/mind connection. It took me ten years of studying Yoga philosophy before I began to feel glimmerings of understanding. I hope to inspire you, with this straightforward cookbook, to enjoy the journey. Check out the "Resources" section at the end of the book for further reading.

2

the

mind

IT WAS THROUGH my yoga practice that I eventually became interested in Ayurveda. I was in search of a holistic health system and a diet that supported my daily practice of poses and breathing. The Ayurvedic diet helped me to maintain my vegetarian values, vigorous exercise, and travel schedule with a sense of strength and enthusiasm. Despite all this, I would still notice the different voices in my head during practice. Confident yoga isn't about listening to self-consciousness and worry (my particular brand of mind fluff). I decided to consult a long-time practitioner about the myth of mental calm through yoga. "Do less physical monkey business and more concentration," he said. "Count your breaths." That sounded awful to me and not in the least glamorous. Yet I practiced counting. The effort to concentrate revealed how active my mind was and how much my thoughts took me away from the present moment. Getting to know my mind, though a little hairy, was the beginning of a path toward peace.

As my yoga practice showed me, the mind is integral to health and happiness. Understanding the mind through the lens of Ayurveda is a spiritual pursuit, and the good news is that you can achieve mental balance through the cultivation of a clear and compassionate observer within. When I practiced counting my breaths, I began to wonder—who is that counting and observing, and who is that telling me that I should be doing something else? So often, we identify with only the turbulent aspects of our minds, because they tend to be the loudest, and we are in the habit of joining their conversation. It takes patience and focus to stay tuned to the calm center, but it is possible. With practice, I stopped listening to the person arguing and began truly concentrating. It was in this state of focus that I finally found calm.

The Ayurvedic diet and lifestyle will steadily strengthen your relationship with your innermost self, the one who sees things as they are and can choose stillness, initiating movement, or resisting change, as appropriate. This flux between stillness and change is balance. To maintain balance in the mind, however, we've got to have a handle on what *mind* means in Ayurveda. Understanding the concept of mind is not only an intellectual pursuit—it is a practical path toward knowing yourself better, which results in feelings of balance, clarity, and lasting happiness.

Understanding the mind is going to take some real-life practice. Let's begin by looking at the mind for what it really is: a subtle object, a process, and a link between body and soul.

the anatomy of mind

In Vedic philosophy, the mind is known as the "inner instrument" of the consciousness that enlivens each of us, while the body is the "outer instrument." The mind experiences, comprehends, and feels. Like the five senses, it is an organ of cognition. Some philosophies state that, because it can sense both the body and consciousness itself, the mind is a bridge between the body and ultimate consciousness, or the soul. If you dissect a brain looking for the mind, you will not find it. Unlike the physical organ of the brain, the mind is composed of subtle energy rather than the five elements. If you studied an ear looking for the sense of hearing, it would be impossible; looking at the hardware of the ear does not reveal the energy that allows the ear to know a sound frequency, to hear.

The anatomy of the mind lies in its different frequencies, or functions. The higher mind comprehends eternal knowledge and universal truths about existence, the middle mind understands sensory experience and emotions, and the lower mind grasps only the physical world. Think of how you experience this range of functions—from inward and subtle, such as creating art or meditating, to outward and earthbound, such as making a shopping list or remembering to pick up some milk. While Western models of the mind relate predominantly to thoughts, emotions, and memories, Vedic philosophy breaks the mind down into four parts that have different frequencies and functions. These functions are thought, comprehension, sensory awareness, and identity. Beyond the mind—linked to it, but not limited by it—is the soul, or pure awareness.

You can cultivate higher frequencies through your food; your activities, such as prayer or selfless service; and where and with whom you hang out. Energy and matter operate on parallel planes that influence each other. For example, think of the energy you cultivate by eating fast food and watching a violent movie versus

---

The Source

— ✦◆✦ —

Information about the mind is found in different places in Ayurvedic texts, but a discussion about the mind falls into the realm of Vedic philosophy, which underlies Ayurveda. For more on this philosophy, start with *Panchadasi*, listed in the "Resources" section, a (relatively!) modern fourteenth-century manual on Advaita Vedanta, one of India's prominent philosophical systems.

cooking a healthy meal at home and reading something inspirational. Our activities create different frequencies in us, and we are influenced by the frequencies of our food and surroundings.

A cornerstone of the sattvic diet is eating foods with high frequencies to cultivate the higher mind and the kind of contentment that comes from feeling connected to a true, universal sense of self (while staying grounded enough to carry on). A food's frequency, or energy, comes from how it is grown, how fresh it is, how it was prepared, and how it is enjoyed. To a lesser degree, the five elements that make up our food also have different frequencies. From the subtle qualities of space to the stable aspects of earth, a well-rounded diet supports all four functions of the mind. When it comes to sattvic cooking, the toolkit comprises an understanding of the energies that are prevalent in your mind and of how your food, through its energy as well as its elements, affects your mind. The term *brain food* takes on a whole new meaning!

MIND MEDICINE: CREATING BALANCE THROUGH FOOD AND ACTIVITIES

The nature of a food, its elemental composition, and the energy surrounding its preparation and consumption will affect the nature of your mind and compel you to act accordingly. That's right, *you act what you eat.* It is through understanding the nature of our food, activities, and relationships that we can effect change on the mind. Remember how the tools work: Ayurveda introduces opposite qualities and reduces similar qualities to achieve a state of balance. If your head is feeling heavy, eat something light composed of space and air. If you are feeling spacey, eat something heavy composed of earth and water. Because the mind is primarily an active system, your activities are especially important in affecting mental energies. If you are feeling overwhelmed, slow down, take a walk, and smell the roses. If you are feeling depressed, get up and move.

The qualities in the table on page 24 will be used throughout the recipe sections to describe the nature of the foods featured. The table describes energies that can manifest in the mind and what kind of foods and activities will amplify each experience (activities are shown in italics). An experience can be decreased by introducing foods or activities of an opposite nature; opposites that balance each other are shown side by side in the table. Practice recognizing these energies. Pay attention to the movements of your mind without judgment, and allow things to make sense slowly in their own time.

Heavy: Heavy foods increase feelings of security and comfort, improve sleep, and decrease anxiety. Examples: milk and cheese, meats, sweet potatoes, *hugging*.

Light: Light foods are energizing and motivating. Examples: raw fruits and vegetables, clear soups, *doing yoga and meditation*.

Dull/slow: Dull foods increase lethargy and/or slow digestion. Examples: ice cream, iced drinks, red meat, pastries, *watching television*.

Sharp/penetrating: Sharp foods give you a wake-up call or increase the appetite. Examples: black pepper, ginger, wasabi, vinegar, alcohol, coffee, lemon, *exercising vigorously, taking an exam*.

Stable: Regular meal times and foods that have grounding effects stabilize the mind and mood. Examples: proteins, dairy, raw nuts, root vegetables, *following a daily routine*.

Mobile/unstable: Skipping meals or eating only light foods leads to unsteadiness in mind and mood. Examples: raw food, caffeine, soft drinks, white sugar, *fasting, traveling*.

Gross: Foods with this quality ground you in the physical body. Examples: animal products, *overeating, oversleeping*.

Subtle: Foods with this quality encourage a spiritual nature. Examples: fresh, organic fruits, vegetables, grains, and legumes; *doing yoga; reading spiritual texts*.

Cloudy: Ever feel socked in by brain fog? That's the cloudy quality at work. Foods that clog the channels increase this feeling. Examples: cold milk and cheese, white flour, trans fats, toxic chemicals, alcohol, pharmaceutical or recreational drugs, *avoiding exercise*.

Clear: A clear head results from foods that digest cleanly and do not leave a residue. Examples: fruits and vegetables with a high water content, clear soups, herbal teas, water, *meditating*.

Cool: Foods that cool the body support a mellow mood. Examples: coconut, cucumber, cilantro, limes, green juices, grapes, melons, *swimming*.

Hot: Foods that heat you up make the mind more stimulated and reactive. Examples: chilies, garlic, raw onion, red wine and spirits, coffee, *participating in competitive sports, debating*.

Moist: The brain is an unctuous organ, and good oils are brain food, lubricating and supporting circulation and longevity. Examples: coconut oil, ghee, sesame oil, *having an oil massage*.

Dry: Foods that promote a dry quality increase anxiety and decrease focus and staying power. Examples: crackers, chips, packaged bars that contain soy, rice "crisps," *exercising excessively*.

understanding balance
and imbalance

Understanding the root causes of imbalance is the key to maintaining health. In Ayurveda, the root causes of diseases can be found in both the body *and* the mind. And you cannot look at the body and mind without their inner compass: the spirit, or soul. This third layer is the seat of stability, balance, and deep happiness. Ayurveda implements physical therapies such as herbal medicines and bodywork, as well as spiritual therapies like meditation, chanting, and prayer to heal the mind. Charaka tells us that these spiritual practices that access the soul are the most effective in remedying disease.

To make food a spiritual therapy, we will have to look at three causes of imbalance. Two of them are rooted in the mind and can greatly affect how we make diet choices if we remain unaware. Interfacing with these aspects of our well-being will help us make wise choices. While this can sound a bit intense, it is amazing to think that with the right foods, eating can become a path to feeling content and happy. We all eat every day, so why not feed the soul as well as fuel the body?

CAUSES OF IMBALANCE

Charaka Samhita tells us that unhappiness results from poor timing and poor use of our mental faculties and five senses. When these three causative factors occur consistently, they lead to imbalance.

- *Kala*: time of day and time of year (seasonal effect)
- *Asatmendriyartha samyoga*: misuse of the sense organs
- *Karma*: actions and activities pertaining to body, speech, and mind that include malfunction of mental faculties and *prajnaparadha* (crimes against wisdom)

Kala. *Kala* means "time," and each of the five elements is most prevalent at certain times of the day, the year, and life. The qualities of these elements as they increase and decrease can cause imbalance. For example, drinking alcohol, eating fried food, and exposing yourself to the midday sun in summer can lead to diseases of pitta, the hot, oily dosha. If you follow a cooling diet in summer, you will encourage optimal health by observing the ideal time of year for enjoying the appropriate balancing foods. Making these wise choices requires a presence of mind that allows you to step back and consider the timing before you act.

Philosophy 101: Satisfaction and Desire

———— ◆◆◆ ————

According to the Yoga system, one basic problem disturbs the mind: a compulsion to look outward, rather than inward, for satisfaction. The mind attaches itself to a "sense object," an object of desire—food, sex, money, power, cars and clothes, and so on—in the false belief that this object will deliver satisfaction. The experience of happiness that depends on an object will ultimately come to an end. True satisfaction, the state of sattva in the mind, is content and unmoved by desire. A steady practice of turning attention *lovingly* inward will uncover this natural state. "Yoga" is considered to be anything that reveals this state of contentment. I'm an advocate for the yoga of food: a practice of cultivating love for the body through true nourishment.

Asatmendriyartha samyoga. *Asatmya* means "incorrect," *indriyas* are the senses, *artha* is the object of the sense organ, and *samyoga* means "to join together." The sense organs are the body parts responsible for the five senses: eyes (sight), ears (hearing), nose (smell), tongue (taste), and skin (touch). Misuse—an incorrect joining of sense organ and object—can mean too much or too little stimulation of the senses but usually means exposing the senses to too much. The nervous system becomes depleted from digesting information from all the sense organs, and the senses may begin to suffer, such as when you have red, dry, itchy eyes after too much screen time or ringing ears after a concert. Bringing the senses back into balance settles the nervous system, thereby reducing stress, which is often the cause of imbalance in the first place. For example, if people with troubled sleep limit their TV, smartphone, or computer time at night, they are more likely to enjoy a good night's rest because they are giving their senses a break. (For suggestions on caring for your senses, see chapter 5.)

Karma. *Karma* means "action." Actions have reactions—if you eat too much fried food, you could end up having diarrhea. *Prajnaparadha*, translated as "crime against intelligence," refers to a mental malfunction that leads to actions with detrimental effects. Knowing from previous experience that fried food will give you diarrhea, you eat it again, and experience the same painful result. Repeating an action that is known to cause suffering seems strange, but it is an aspect of human nature—one that has been going on for a few thousand years, according to Ayurvedic texts. The term "crime against intelligence" speaks to a misuse of our intellect where we take an action that does not reflect our natural smarts. The intellect knows the difference between helpful and harmful, yet a desire is so alluring that we go for it anyway. It's helpful to note that when your body or mind is in a state of imbalance, your cravings will reflect that imbalance, and vice versa. The imbalance itself does the talking, and in this case, errant desires can set the stage for disease. As your body/mind comes back into balance, your cravings will begin to reflect natural intelligence again. In the earlier example of fried food, we may choose heavy food in an attempt to slow down an overactive mind or "make up for" a busy day. Enjoying some downtime with a self-massage could be a better way to ease the mind and alleviate those heavy/fried food cravings.

A balanced, sattvic mind naturally makes healthy choices. The three causative factors can, over time, begin to obscure this state of clear perception. Pausing to consider the best time for an action and taking care how we use our senses and mental faculties will help us stay centered and retain clarity in the mind.

Prajnaparadha: A Case Study in Emotional Eating

— ◆ ◆ ◆ —

I'm a huge brownie fan. It has taken me years to enjoy one brownie without eating the whole pan. When I was feeling lonely, sad, or stressed out, I would lose the connection to my centered, clear, and contented self. I would look for the present moment to feel *different*. I wanted to feel whole, happy, and relaxed. Enter the pan of brownies. My mind would remember the experience of eating a brownie and how pleasing it was. In pursuit of that pleasure, I used to reach for the treat. Sadly, when I finished eating, my sense of taste soon forgot the pleasure, and I would be right back where I started. Or even worse, I would feel the brownie sitting in my gut or crash from the temporary sugar high. As my mind's natural clarity became gummed up by overeating, I adopted a destructive, defeated attitude that led to eating more brownies and perpetuated the cycle of momentary pleasure and heavy, dull aftereffect.

Why did my mind remember only the pleasure and not the complete story—aka, the unsatisfying ending? The flawed mind process here is prajnaparadha. The mind's truthful processing of information and memory was usurped by an even more compelling pursuit of pleasure. Desire can do that, and when the call of a craving becomes strong enough, it takes a strong mind to override it. Had I used a more balanced approach to the emotions of loneliness and stress, such as taking a bath for self-care or closely investigating the emotion through journaling or meditation, I would have created more comfort and balance in the long run. It takes time, effort, and experience to make intelligent choices consistently. But once you feel the results, wise choices get easier, and new habits replace the old.

Still want a brownie? Not a problem. Just understand the brownie is going to be gone at some point, and be OK with that. It is not the experience of brownie pleasure that makes problems; it is the compelling desire to repeat the pleasurable experience that gets us in trouble. *It is not the brownie you are after, but the experience of pleasure, which is available with or without the treat.*

mental digestion: agni, tejas, and prana

I am the most careful about my diet when life gets busy. I have noticed that if I take on too much or don't eat the right combination of nourishing and vitalizing foods, it feels like my mind can't keep up, and it begins to shut down, leaving me feeling sleepy and sad. At other times, I have reacted to busyness by overdoing caffeine and putting the pedal to the metal, ending up anxious and sleepless. These times of managing what life is throwing at me have taught me the importance of mental digestion, and I take great care to preserve the fires of my mind through a nourishing diet and a conscious lifestyle.

Let's take a peek under the hood at the workings of our mental digestion, an important player in maintaining a balanced mind. Just as clean, complete digestion is the number-one requirement for disease prevention and the health of your body, the same is true for your mind. Strong mental digestion breaks down the daily influx of sensory information and experience to avoid buildup (mental toxins) and overload, which lead to anxiety, anger, or depression. When the mental faculties are all running smoothly, there is space in the mind for pure awareness (your true nature) to really shine.

When we look under the hood, we find *agni* and *prana*, the fire and the air that stokes the fire. These powers aid mental digestion by processing our emotions and life experiences (that is, the "information" of our internal world). Any emotion you feel—excitement about an upcoming event, love, or anger—must be broken into digestible bits, accepted and absorbed, or processed and eliminated. Our experiences, just like our food, require digestion. This is why we get tired in the evening—too much input! Dreaming is one of the ways the mind processes the experiences of the day.

AGNI AND TEJAS

Agni ("UG-nee"), the fire element, resides principally in the stomach where the body's main fire, the *jathara agni*, is. Here, the food that has been chewed and mixed with saliva is transformed into the building blocks of the body. But fire also pervades the entire body, providing the heat necessary for transformation. This heat and transformation fills the mind with light. *Tejas* ("TAY-jus") is the essence of fire that continues to metabolize after the initial breakdown and keeps the mind sharp and bright. Think of tejas as the sustained glow of fire, whereas agni is blazing heat. A luminous "inner glow" does not come just from fire in the body; it requires a bright consciousness as well.

An illuminated mind is a state of overall clarity and, dare I say, en*light*enment. Bringing things to light is what healthy mental digestion does, without a buzz of confusion or a cloudy fog of emotion. Imagine creating an invention or a scientific breakthrough—the neurons are firing in your brain, blazing new pathways of fresh ideas and deeper understanding. Imagine feeling mentally sharp, on cue, and creative. Brilliant. This is a result of tejas.

Interestingly, a brilliant mental state begins with the digestion of food. It goes both ways: strong digestion promotes clarity of the physical body, and a clear, undisturbed mind allows for complete digestion. (Think of how you feel after a meal when you are angry. Acid stomach?) You cannot separate the gut from the mind; therefore, keeping the digestive fire strong may be the number-one thing to consider in the shared health of mind and body. The ancient practice of eating easily digestible foods and digestive spices at the appropriate time and in the right amounts will ensure healthy agni. Health, stamina, and luster begin in the stomach.

THE WORKINGS OF AGNI, PRANA, AND TEJAS

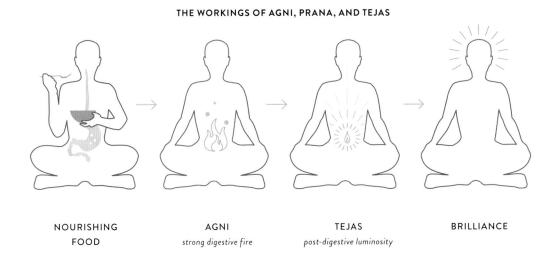

NOURISHING
FOOD

AGNI
strong digestive fire

TEJAS
post-digestive luminosity

BRILLIANCE

Spotlight on Ama: The Agni-Blocker

—— ◆ ◆ ◆ ——

Since clarity of mind and gut are inextricably linked, we have to talk about *ama* ("AAH-ma"), the anti-agni. When food doesn't break down completely due to less-than-ideal food choices or eating practices and/or stress, ama begins. It is a thick, sticky, leftover substance that sits in the stomach and smothers the digestive fire, precipitating more ama from future meals. This result of incomplete digestion can dull and slow the mind as well as the body.

If these factors continue for a while, ama begins to travel from the stomach through the rest of the body, gunking up the channels of circulation and nutrition, the organs, and so on. Ama likes to stick around anywhere there is a weak spot, as in the case of joint inflammation or chronic congestion. Once ama is in the tissues, everything slows down—not only the system or organ where the toxins are, but everything—including the mind. This toxic situation can be responsible for the common complaint of brain fog, especially when you notice it soon after meals. Modifying food choices and habits, or undergoing a detoxification period, can clear this up. The remedy is to make space and encourage digestion of the backlog. Note to self: clearing ama from the digestive tract is way easier than clearing it from the deeper tissues. Luckily, the recipes and lifestyle guidelines in this book will teach you how to keep your gut healthy, reducing the chance of deep-seated ama.

Ama Checklist

—— ◆ ◆ ◆ ——

If you *consistently* experience several of the following, you may have ama.

- Opaque, white coating on the tongue that doesn't scrape off
- Bad taste in the mouth, bad breath
- Sinus or lung congestion
- Grogginess after meals
- Heavy, sticky, stinky stools
- Strong body odor
- Lymphatic congestion (swelling such as swollen breasts before periods or bloating after meals)
- Constipation and/or diarrhea
- Low libido
- Mental confusion (brain fog)
- Persistent sadness or negative outlook

If you think you have ama, check out appendix 2 for a three-day mind-cleanse as a starting point to burning it off. Better yet, consult an Ayurvedic practitioner for a personal detox plan.

PRANA: LIFE ENERGY

Prana ("PRAAH-nah"), like the air element, is always moving. Its current enlivens the
sense organs and the field of thought. Pranic energy fuels the functions of agni and
tejas. When you build a fire, you have to blow on it to get it going. Proper circulation
of prana ensures a steady intellectual flame. To illuminate an idea through speech or
art, prana is the energy of the mind that is required to start moving and stay focused.

This is life energy—an organism without prana is dead. A body without prana is
only a mash-up of the five elements with nothing moving at all. This energy circulates
around your body, carried by the currents of the air element and the movements of
your attention. A break in prana's rhythmic circulation can be physical, like cholesterol
blocking an artery, gas sticking in the intestines, or a general disconnect from the
physical body (such as all computer, no exercise). However, psychic causes such as
chronic stress, worry, or grief can also disturb the circulation of prana.

Stress may be as important as physical causes in the modern progression of diseases. There is a common Ayurvedic saying: "Where the attention goes, prana flows."
Think of how persistent worry can occupy your mind. Stress is a huge drain on life
energy. Whatever you pay attention to, it receives your energy. For example, sending
kind energy to an injured knee versus ignoring it and pushing through the pain will
create healing or perpetuate the injury, respectively. In our busy day-to-day lives, it
is easy to lose touch with the movements of life energy and attention and to end up
worrying or working all the time. It takes practice, but a slow and steady commitment
to paying attention to self-care and self-love pays off in the prana bank. Ayurveda
abounds with rejuvenating routines for all seasons and stages of life.

The seat of prana is "the spiritual heart," according to Ayurveda. This heart resides in the center of the chest, not off to the side like the muscular heart. The next time you hold a loved one or a really cute puppy, feel for the center of your chest. There it is. Even better, the next time you notice yourself stressing, go hug that puppy. Cultivating a connection to spirit—whether through the natural world, meditation, religion, puppies, or whatever works for you—is the main line to feeling full power. By connecting to the spiritual nature of your mind and your life, you connect to an infinite source of energy—far greater than you will find in the body alone.

A Breathing Exercise

— ◆ ◆ —

As part of an Ayurvedic lifestyle, the art and science of yoga is excellent for cultivating and circulating prana. The channel through which prana enters the body is the nostrils, hence yoga's use of nasal breathing. Breathing rhythmically through the nose while moving is a wonderful longevity practice. Be sure to practice yoga in such a way that your breath enters through your nose and retains an unbroken rhythm, or there is little benefit. An experienced yoga teacher will be able to help you establish a rhythmic breath in movement.

At home, you can try this seated breathing practice. In a chair or any comfortable seat where you can straighten your spine and gently lift your chest, begin counting to four as you inhale through your nose, then again count to four while you exhale through your nose. To help you stay focused, you can touch the tip of each finger to your thumb as you inhale, beginning with the index finger and working across to the pinkie. On your fourth breath cycle, when you exhale at the pinkie, begin to work your way back to the index finger. Repeat this three to five times, or set an alarm for five minutes. Slowly increase your time to increase the relaxation benefits.

BUILDING YOUR MENTAL MUSCLES

Applying your mind to the act of mental digestion promotes a state of mental balance and increases the strength of your mind. According to Ayurveda, a "strong mind" is one that remains in equanimity (unperturbed) despite the ebb and flow of daily life. The strong-minded are able to "go with the flow" patiently, as well as make clear choices and actions when necessary.

Obviously, this takes a lot of practice and life experience. Sufficient rest, yoga, and meditation/contemplation will greatly increase the body's ability to process experience and emotion efficiently by bringing prana to the mental muscles. Remember, where the attention goes, prana flows, so anything that brings attention to the activity of the mind will make the mind stronger. Being too busy and never looking within will eventually overwhelm the mind and lead to overactive thoughts, stress, and worry. Think of overdoing in your daily life as you would think of overdoing at a buffet. It's OK on occasion, but stuffing yourself regularly will overwhelm your system. On the flip side, a lethargic mind that avoids emotion or experience can lead to various states of dullness or depression.

For your everyday approach to strong mental digestion, set the stage for a balanced mind by eating a diet that builds agni and prana and that reduces ama. All the recipes and information in this book will get you started.

Mind Benders

——— ◆ ◆ ◆ ———

In considering what the mind is, it's important to note what the mind *isn't*. Mainly, the mind isn't *you*. It is a very busy aspect of you and can be quite convincing in telling you that its thoughts are the most important thing going. Beginning to know yourself as more than a mind is the path toward balance. Let's deconstruct a few common misconceptions and consider their Ayurvedic solutions.

1. YOUR BRAIN IS NOT YOUR MIND

The brain is a fatty, jelly-like organ inside the skull that weighs about three pounds. It is responsible for motor functions like balance, autonomic functions like breathing, interpretation of the information brought in by the sense organs, and storage (memory).

Ayurveda references the mind as separate from the brain. It is a subtle object, composed predominantly of subtle energies—just because you can't see them, doesn't mean they're not there. Mind is responsible for the movements of attention. For example, when you look at a tree, your attention is pixilated; your attention moves from place to place all around the tree, putting together an image of what you are looking at. The mind sees one point at a time but moves from point to point *very quickly*. Then the mind might make a judgment about whether or not the tree is a pretty one, needs more water, or reminds you of a tree that was in your grandmother's yard. All this happens in less than a minute and happens without you trying or even noticing.

2. *YOU* ARE NOT YOUR MIND

If you practice the exercise of observing the mind taking in a tree, or any object, you are practicing *awareness*. Awareness transcends the mind and can observe the mind's functions. Awareness can recognize the activity of the sense organs and thoughts; notice feelings like desire or repulsion; and know itself as separate from these thoughts, activities, and feelings. The philosophy and practice of Yoga involves getting to know this observer, the self who is aware of thoughts and feelings. In a state of mental confusion, human beings identify with thoughts and feelings and lose their sense of perspective.

In this misinformed state, thoughts and feelings run the show. With the practice of awareness, we begin to identify with the higher mind. In this state, a sense of calm and peace presides, despite the compelling presence of thoughts and feelings.

3. *YOU* ARE NOT YOUR BODY

The Charaka Samhita tells us that "body, senses, mind, and soul are the four components of Ayu; without their constant connection, Ayur [life] cannot exist." The body is, in most cases, where we look when we think about wellness, but what about the more subtle pieces of the whole? Ayurveda works on all four of these levels to establish a holistic sense of well-being. Leave one out, and wellness will be elusive. We are looking specifically at how our food and daily routines link to the health of the senses, mind, and soul. The soul is universal and transcends the body. It is the part in each of us that connects to a larger, deeper sense of reality and is the seat of our love, intuition, and discernment. That's important stuff.

The five-element synergy that makes up the manifest universe, including our physical selves, is illuminated by consciousness. Each cell has consciousness. Your body didn't have to go to food school to know food goes in the mouth and comes out the back door; a white blood cell didn't go to cell school to know how to be a working part of the bloodstream. To be a working part of this "life stream" requires a connection to your higher consciousness. When connected to the essence of *you* beyond only the body, you feel satisfaction, stability, and a deeper meaning in life.

4. *YOU* ARE THE TRUE-YOU

It is a common mistake to believe that the mind and body, and their thoughts and feelings, are what and who we really are. This misconception is a cause of disease, and it happens when thoughts and feelings run the show. Choices made from a vantage point of attachment, greed, anger, pride, depression, and so on can get us into trouble. For example, when I'm feeling sad and have the impulse to eat brownies, I have learned to check in with myself first. My true self knows from experience that brownies will not solve my sadness. When I make the choice to eat one or not, it then comes from the true-me, not from sad-me. "True-you" is a moment-by-moment process. There are no right and wrong choices, only opportunities to return to the pure awareness at your center. And *that* is who you really are.

3

the

maha gunas

MENTAL ENERGIES

WHEN IT IS TIME TO BEGIN A PROJECT—whether it's writing a book or cleaning the kitchen—you gather your energy and begin to focus on the task. Once you get your work off the ground, the momentum takes over, and you are on a roll. Eventually, you begin to feel tired, lose focus, and slow down; then you take a rest from the project. When your energy returns, you gear up and begin work again. This natural ebb and flow of energy is in motion all the time. Even when we are still, we are preparing to move again. The dynamic interplay of potential energy, kinetic energy, and inertia is omnipresent.

The *maha gunas* are three threads, interwoven by the laws of nature, that comprise the energies of existence. You may remember from chapter 1 that they consist of sattva (light and clarity); rajas (movement and change); and tamas (inertia and darkness). These aspects of energy are present in everything, as the light of a new day moves into activity, then gives way to darkness at night. They are creation, preservation, and destruction, mirrored by the Hindu deities Brahma, the Creator; Vishnu, the Sustainer; and Shiva, the Destroyer. These energies govern the movements of all life, including the mind. The essential energy of the mind is sattva, a clear space of truth, contentment, and stability. The energies of rajas and tamas act on this space. Rajas increases movement in the mind, while tamas slows it down.

Happily, sattva can be preserved by eating fresh, organic foods and by engaging in activities that promote harmony, like yoga, meditation, and time in nature. Rajas increases with excessive use of spicy, sour foods, and activities that cause movement in the body or mind, such as video games and competitive sports. Tamas increases with the intake of old and processed foods and activities that dull the mind, like too much TV or using drugs and alcohol.

Just like with the three doshas, a harmonious relationship among the maha gunas is the key to mental wellness. In a balanced state, the mind sees things clearly and accepts them as they are, but it can instigate and resist changes when appropriate. The right amount of change brings stability as well as empowerment.

Without the maha gunas (the energies of our world), all matter would be inert. The interplay of the three *gunas* underlies the material nature of the world and of human beings. *Guna* means "quality," and there are three basic qualities to the energies of nature, including human nature:

Sattva: the energy of satisfaction, illumination, clarity, harmony
Rajas: the energy of movement, change, creativity, passion
Tamas: the energy of rest, inertia, stagnation, destruction

Maha means "great," so these are the three biggies, describing the qualities of nature's energy—not to be confused with the physical "twenty gunas," which are qualities used to describe foods and medicines. Without three gunas, we would all just sit, totally inanimate. The universe as we know it would not exist. Newton's apple is a great example of these energies at play—growing on the tree, undergoing inescapable changes, eventually slowing and falling to decay on the ground. The maha gunas are one way of describing the fundamental laws of nature.

The nature of consciousness is pure, undisturbed sattva. The word *sat* may be translated as "to be," which makes *sattva* simply a "state of pure being." Simple as Newton's apple growing on the tree. The mind, however, is a complex instrument designed to comprehend the internal self and the external environment and ultimately to bridge the two. In Ayurveda, mental wellness is patient and alert, we are able to both accept things as they are and take necessary actions for preservation and prosperity. Our thoughts and desires move through the mental field, but balanced consciousness sees them for what they are and discerns when to act and when to remain still—without angst, anxiety, or regret. Our sattvic mind is an unbiased observer, not troubled by agendas or cravings.

"Untroubled by agendas or cravings"—doesn't that sound nice? I'll take two! The thing is, the gunas are always acting on one another, and this dynamic dance is what makes the world go around and allows for creativity and change.

THE DOSHAS OF THE MIND

Rajas and tamas are known as the "doshas of the mind." We could also call them "doshas of sattva." Sattva is the pure state of the mind, and rajas and tamas are the energies that disturb it. *It's important to note that—like vata, pitta, and kapha doshas—rajas and tamas are necessary, functional aspects of our existence.* The mind has to move, and it has to slow down. Rajas and tamas aren't "bad" per se, they just have a trickster energy and a tendency toward imbalance when we aren't paying attention. *Dosha*, or "that which is faulty," refers to the states of rajas and tamas that occur when these energies have accumulated beyond the point of balance. It is certainly human nature to experience imbalance sometimes, but it helps to be mindful of some of the telltale signs and symptoms.

Unlike the body's constitution of the five elements (which is fixed at birth), the qualities in your mind can change over your lifetime. While it is true that the hot nature of the fire element, for example, can cause rajasic tendencies in the mind, or the heavy, slow nature of earth and water can cause a propensity toward tamas, *your elemental constitution does not necessarily lead to a particular guna in the mind.*

The mind is stronger than matter, and balanced gunas can remain harmonious despite elemental imbalance. Even if your body is sick, your mind can still be well.

Just as it is not helpful to self-identify as a physical dosha ("I'm so vata"), it is not helpful to consider yourself "rajasic" or "tamasic"; it is better to encourage a harmonious dance between the three gunas in your mind. Remember the gunas are interwoven and part of our fundamental nature, so expecting to experience sattva all the time would, itself, be a state of imbalance.

Cultivation of sattva naturally brings your mind back to its satisfied state of union with your true self and calms rajas. Tamas requires the activity of rajas to mobilize stagnation, lifting the mind from darkness into the serenity of sattva.

As you learn about the three gunas and how diet and activities affect them, you may notice patterns in yourself—in the direction of too much (cool your jets!) or too little (attention, couch potatoes) mental movement. This can be helpful information and does not make you irredeemably too passionate or too mellow. There are no "bad" choices, just opportunities to discover patterns within yourself. With this self-awareness, you can discover Ayurveda's many tools for balancing the energies of your mind, ranging from diet to playtime to meditation. We will touch on a number of them throughout this book. With steady observation and practice, you will begin to notice changes.

The Roots of Mental Trends

—— ◆ ◆ ◆ ——

Leaning toward either rajas or tamas in your mental sphere can be greatly influenced by your habits. For example, a client came to see me because he had trouble falling asleep at night. I saw a connection between the loud, busy household where he grew up and the fact that he finds himself now drawn toward a loud, busy lifestyle of working too much, hanging out at bars, and texting all the time. We noted how the quality of energy he is accustomed to compels him to seek out the familiar. Like increases like, and after living his twenties "out loud," at thirty-three, the mental clamor was keeping him up at night. I suggested daily walks in the evening without a phone, noticing the natural world all around him. He felt the difference at bedtime, and as the introduction of *quiet* began to change the nature of his mind, he began to crave quiet walks and sometimes even chose to take them instead of going to the sports bar. Simple tools and changes like this can be incredibly effective.

SATTVAVAJAYA: HEALING THE MIND

Sattvavajaya means "victory over the mind" and refers to a branch of Ayurvedic psychology that includes techniques for healing the mind and emotions. Therapies can be diet; herbs; bodywork; meditation and yoga; and lifestyle choices that foster a connection between heart, mind, and self. Remember, the seat of the mind is in the spiritual heart, and both mind and heart must digest and metabolize emotions to retain clarity in mind and moods. It is a process to ensure that victory and not something that comes effortlessly. The Charaka Samhita notes that the most important quality in this process is patience, and it requires willingness to look within for the deepest truth in all matters.

Healing the mind may sound a bit lofty, but truthfully, Ayurveda will meet you wherever you are. While the study of the maha gunas reveals the movements of the mind to the keen observer, this knowledge can also inform decisions about your food and daily routine. Changes to your routine can change both your body and your mind—transforming your overall health. From simple dietary changes that improve your physical well-being to managing irritability or sadness, it all counts. All realms of life are fertile ground for self-transformation. I recommend you work with what feels right at this particular time, and don't worry about the rest. Maybe you will come back to some of the deeper aspects of being later on. Maybe not. You can trust that Ayurveda will take you in the right direction when it is your time.

Practice Note: As you consider turning your attention to the activity of your mind, it's a good idea to line up some help in navigating these psychological waters. Be sure to have adequate support from a like-minded community, spiritual guidance, or an experienced teacher or counselor as you are starting out.

Many references to sattva, rajas, and tamas appear in the Bhagavad Gita, an epic poem that is between two thousand and five thousand years old. The title means "Song of God" or "Song of the Universe." This poem is like a guidebook for all walks of life, explaining the Yogic lifestyle, and goes in depth on how to balance the three gunas through beneficial food choices, dharma (following our own unique path), and acts of love. This systematic path of living our unique truth is called Yoga.

what is sattva?

"Sattva, being pure, is illuminating and free from misery."
—THE BHAGAVAD GITA

Purity is a simple thing. It is a state in which the mind expands beyond all the daily chatter—worry, stress, chores, the "small stuff." The mental faculties quiet down, relax, and expand, like your muscles do when you lie in a bath. When the mind expands, it merges with the universe, whose qualities are expansive, including the sky, stars, and planets. There is a sense of trust and communion, like resting your soul in the cosmic bathtub.

Sattva is an experiential thing. I picture the *rishis*, the sages of ancient India, as professional meditators, supported by society in penetrating the mysteries of life. All of the information we have on the maha gunas comes from these ancient sages. Bright-eyed and bushy-tailed at the age of nineteen, I set off on a mystical journey to India to seek this ancient knowledge. My plan was to return a "yoga teacher." I learned a lot of things, mainly how much I *didn't* understand and how prone to distraction I was. True understanding takes a solid attention span, and that took me years to begin (I'm still working on it). However, on a weeklong retreat up in the Himalayas, eating sattvic food and studying ancient texts with a good teacher and a like-minded community, I had a moment of blissful illumination. Sitting on a mountaintop, I felt myself expand and merge with the cosmos. It began at my heart and spread. Almost instantly, the realization of what was happening came through the mind-field, with fear on its heels. Some part of my mind felt an earthquake coming and contracted back into my body. Since then, it has happened a few times, and after two decades, I can say a blissful state is possible. I believe *anybody* can connect to this state by opening the mind. Bliss can illuminate and inform day-to-day life, and the cultivation of an expansive mind is the ticket.

We all have a mind-field, and we purposefully fill it with stuff. We fill it with billboards, shiny gadgets, small talk, regrets, and anxieties. It can sometimes feel like the day-to-day is designed to make us forget the truth. Truth is simple. When the mind identifies with its infinite energy source, life is buoyant. If you are drawing from this limitless well, you will notice your mind and moods are resilient, steady.

In this sattvic state, you will feel OK with what you are doing rather than thinking you should be doing something else. You will prefer to see and accept the truth, not react to or deny it. From the cosmic hopper, concentration will come easily, as will simple love and kindness for yourself, others, and the environment.

SIGNS OF SATTVIC MIND

These signs of sattva will take some time to develop, but it is helpful to know where you are headed. As you begin integrating a practice tip or two, use this list to watch for signposts along the way:

- An ability to concentrate, as well as to calmly shift your attention
- Self-confidence
- Sound sleep
- Healthy cravings
- Sustained energy
- Emotional stability

DIET AND LIFESTYLE TO CULTIVATE SATTVA

Foods that cultivate sattva are fresh, seasonal, lovingly prepared, simple, and nourishing. Whole grains, nuts and seeds, legumes, fresh fruits, and vegetables are the staples of a sattvic diet. Activities to promote sattva include all things contemplative and outdoorsy: meditation, cooking, gardening, arts and crafts, hiking, conscious communication, the giving of gifts, and volunteer and service work.

> **PRACTICE TIP:** Continuously remind yourself that your energy comes from a universal source, and practice connecting to that source. Pausing to take three deep breaths before a meal is a great time to connect. In time, your body knows this experience so well that it becomes second nature, and mealtimes become touchstones in a busy day.

what is rajas?

Imagine me back on the mountaintop in the Himalayas. I have too much coffee one morning. I wrap in my shawl, sit on the rock, and my mind starts bouncing everywhere. I can't sit still, my foot keeps tapping, my hands are shaking, and I have to go to the bathroom. Then I start thinking about all the things I have to do that day. There went that opportunity for blissful expansion. Instead, I decide to harness the creative energy of rajas and do some writing.

Yes, we all need rajas, the energy of movement, creativity, and change that can be harnessed for new projects, exciting plans, material success, and even self-transformation. But it's strong stuff—passionate, driven, and excitable. Rajas can have a tendency to move *too much*. In a rajasic state of mind, we might swing between hyperactivity and hyperfocus, leaning toward extremes. In excess, intense motivation becomes imbalanced energies like restlessness, obsession, or perfectionism. The associated emotions can be turbulent, overwhelming, and impatient. Rajasic energy can lead to rash, thoughtless acts or a competitive, critical, or self-serving attitude. In the long term, this hypermode leads to exhaustion and anxiety, and eventually the inertia of tamas sets in.

SIGNS AND SYMPTOMS OF RAJASIC MIND

While it is wonderful to have some zing, too much of the rajasic qualities can make you feel a little worked up. If they predominate in your life for too long, you might start to notice the following:

- Difficulty falling asleep, or waking up in the wee hours
- Racing thoughts
- An inability to sit still
- Workaholism
- Cravings for spicy food, alcohol, and stimulants

DIET AND LIFESTYLE TO CALM RAJAS

Foods that increase rajas in the mind are spicy, sour, salty, heating, and stimulating. Drinking alcohol, ingesting caffeine, smoking, working too much, traveling, and having too much sex are lifestyle choices that increase rajas.

Foods that decrease rajas are naturally sweet, freshly prepared, soothing to the body, and delicately flavorful, such as fresh herbs and spices; juicy, sweet fruits; and root vegetables. Activities that calm the mind and slow the pace also reduce rajas. They may include time in nature, meditation, gentle yoga, swimming, free time, time with loved ones, and volunteer work.

what is tamas?

Imagine I am back on the mountaintop in the Himalayas, but our group took a long hike the day before. My body is tired. I stumble out of bed, wrap myself in a shawl, sit on the rock, and begin to nod off. The mellow energy of tamas is present to balance yesterday's activity. This is a great opportunity to rest now and meditate later.

In balance, the gravity of tamas brings sound sleep, a desire to rest, and an appreciation for creature comfort. This all sounds great, but in excess, this gravity can become a deadweight that leads to depression, inactivity, and dullness. Tamas is heavy, slow, stubborn, unmotivated, and sleepy. The corresponding emotions can be sadness, lack of self-esteem, hopelessness, and fear. A tamasic mind gets stuck and has a difficult time getting started, clearing, or seeing the bright side of things. This lethargic energy needs to be excited by the activity of rajas in order to eventually move into a balanced state.

SIGNS AND SYMPTOMS OF TAMASIC MIND

- Hopelessness
- Brain fog
- Oversleeping
- Loss of appetite or cravings for fried or processed foods

DIET AND LIFESTYLE TO MOTIVATE TAMAS

Certain activities and foods increase one or more tamasic symptoms, whereas others will help to lighten the heavy load. Foods that increase tamas are old, stale, soggy, left-over, microwaved, deep-fried, greasy, heavy, canned, frozen (more than a week or two), denatured/processed, artificial, or overcooked dishes. Activities that increase tamas include watching TV (especially violence), trolling social media, sitting around, sleeping in the daytime, and overeating. It is important to note that it is the buildup of too much of any of these factors that makes a problem—a bit of heavy food and sitting around may be just what the doctor ordered from time to time.

Foods that decrease tamas are fresh, light, local, and vegetarian. Activities that decrease tamas include anything uplifting, especially yoga, dancing, singing and chanting, reading inspiring or spiritual materials, and time outside.

Balancing the energies of the mind takes practice. Through awareness, you can recognize the early signs of imbalance, and this will allow you to come back to center sooner. Only when an imbalance has been around for a while does it progress to affecting your overall well-being. The following table lists common, early signs of imbalance in the mind, how to recognize them, and a key action to move back toward a state of mental balance.

Remember, this is a judgment-free zone. These signs of imbalance are common and nothing to beat yourself up about. Keep a sense of humor, and simply begin by noticing if you are experiencing any of these signs. They indicate how you might be able to adapt your diet or lifestyle.

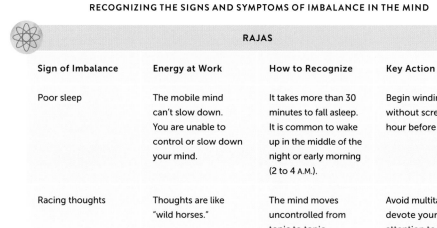

RAJAS			
Sign of Imbalance	**Energy at Work**	**How to Recognize**	**Key Action**
Poor sleep	The mobile mind can't slow down. You are unable to control or slow down your mind.	It takes more than 30 minutes to fall asleep. It is common to wake up in the middle of the night or early morning (2 to 4 A.M.).	Begin winding down, without screens, one hour before bedtime.
Racing thoughts	Thoughts are like "wild horses."	The mind moves uncontrolled from topic to topic, without finishing any particular train of thought.	Avoid multitasking; devote your full attention to one thing at a time to cultivate concentration.
Irritability	You are hot-headed, quick to react, and always in a hurry.	Little things begin to cause anger. You experience road rage and are impatient when waiting in lines.	Start by just noticing aggravation and impatience. Remind yourself there is time, and everything is OK. Slow your breath.
Loss of concentration	The mind darts around from object to object.	Be aware of multi-tasking. Has the mind forgotten how to attend to each activity fully?	Practice looking at an object, like a tree or flower, for a few minutes. Set a timer. Observe the object and try to keep your attention there.
Tension headaches	Headaches seem to come out of nowhere but actually begin with tension in the jaw, eyes, neck, or shoulders. They can result from worry and stress.	When something is worrying you, check in with your jaw, eyes, and neck. Give your body permission to relax.	Get to know your own early signs of tension. Foam rolling the upper back helps with headaches resulting from neck tension.
Inability to sit still	Your body is restless, like you want to jump out of your skin.	Watch for jiggling feet, nail biting, and fidgeting.	Once you begin noticing fidgets, practice consciously stopping the activity in the moment—over and over again.

TAMAS

Sign of Imbalance	Energy at Work	How to Recognize	Key Action
Brain fog	You have difficulty engaging or maintaining attention. You are always sleepy.	There is a heavy sensation in your head, especially the eyes. This can correspond with a heavy feeling in the entire body and a desire to sleep.	Move your body until the fog breaks up: take a long walk, have a dance party, etc.
Loss of appetite	You have a heavy feeling in your stomach and no excitement for mealtimes.	Healthy foods have little appeal.	Sip hot water, ginger tea, or Vitalitea. Do not eat until you're hungry.
Procrastination	You experience difficulty in getting started but are better once things are moving.	Notice how you talk yourself out of getting started on something new. Are you overwhelmed, self-deprecating, or not interested?	Get to know your flavor of "not-doing" and begin to smile at the inner conversation that tries to keep you from beginning.
Lethargy	You are bored or exhausted.	Activities that used to excite you no longer do. Your main desire is to lie around or indulge only in sedentary activities.	Get up and move. In the event you are over-tired, practice taking rest until the feeling subsides. Ask yourself if the exhaustion comes from tamasic food or overwork.
Difficulty making decisions	You hem and haw, questioning yourself.	You second-guess yourself, are unable to follow through with anything, and feel tension in your body.	Get to know the difference between mental chatter and intuition. Intuition sounds calm and slow and is easy to trust. Chatter is fast and insecure.
Resistance to change	You dig your heels in and are often a stick in the mud.	You cling to what you know, such as comfort foods and familiar faces and places. You have a fear of new people and places.	Try being spontaneous! Go somewhere you've never been, try something new—start with something fun.

4

food
and
mind

A STRONG, HEALTHY MIND comes from a daily practice of enjoying a simple, wholesome diet and lifestyle. You will notice that most Ayurvedic recommendations for meals and activities emphasize the beauty of simplicity. In true form, the cultivation of sattva through food is a simple concept. Food that is fresh, local, and lovingly prepared is full of prana and brings energy to the body and mind. When food is natural, it fosters a connection to the natural world. When food is denatured, it eventually leads to a sense of separateness from the universe. Distorted tastes and colors, as well as chemicals, in our food distort our mental energies over time.

The five elements are the material nature of our world and the key to maintaining balance through food. Ayurveda employs the qualities of all six tastes—each taste a combination of two elements—to ensure balance in both body and mind. It is a diet that habitually favors only certain tastes that can get us into trouble. Naturally sweet foods, such as whole grains, legumes, and root vegetables, combined with smaller amounts of the other five tastes, preserve the mind's natural state of balance. In this chapter, we will look at the six tastes and how they affect the mind.

Exploring a sattvic diet is a great place to start on the path to mental balance, and this diet includes not only what you eat, but *how* you eat. Even the freshest, most lovingly prepared food loses its beneficial effects when eaten in a hurry. In the following pages, I offer suggestions for promoting mental balance by choosing sattvic foods, as well as by maintaining a simple and thoughtful environment while cooking and eating. By taking a little time to enjoy wholesome foods in a nurturing environment, you will be well on your way to promoting a strong, healthy mind.

shad rasa: the six tastes

The Sanskrit word for taste is *rasa*. It is such a cool word—it means "sap or juice." In Ayurvedic medicine, this juice is known as *rasa dhatu*, meaning blood plasma and lymphatic tissue (fluid, lymph nodes, and associated lymphatic organs) that circulate all over the body maintaining proper immune function—truly the sap of life.

In the Hindu arts, *rasa* means "essence, flavor, or mood." This is considered the most important quality to be transmitted through music and dance, literature, and visual arts. I studied Indian classical dance for a few years, at one point learning the facial cues for the rasa of delight, laughter, sorrow, anger, energy, fear, disgust, heroism, and astonishment. A pinnacle of the human experience is to "taste" these different flavors of emotion.

The six tastes in Ayurveda describe not only the flavors of different foods, but their vital essence as well. This vital essence then yields its particular qualities to the body/mind after digestion. Think of each taste as a group of qualities derived from two elements. For example, sweet taste brings the moist, soft, juicy qualities of earth and water, and it is equated to the experience of love.

A food gets its qualities from the dominant elements and can often exhibit more than one taste. It's intuitive: a food with more water will feel moist, while something fiery will have a kick. You will notice that the taste usually indicates a food's health properties. For example, earthy, sweet food smooths agitation, and fiery food burns out dullness. The recipes in this book use the tastes therapeutically, and you will find that incorporating different tastes in the right amounts at the right time will keep you feeling steady in both body and mind. *It is the balance of all six tastes that sustains the mental equilibrium of sattva.* In the case of rajas, fiery tastes like hot peppers will be reduced. In the case of tamas, bitter and astringent tastes like leafy greens, as well as fiery tastes, will be increased.

THE SIX TASTES AND THEIR ELEMENTS

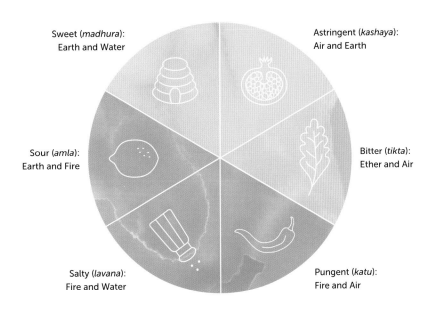

Sweet (*madhura*):
Earth and Water

Astringent (*kashaya*):
Air and Earth

Sour (*amla*):
Earth and Fire

Bitter (*tikta*):
Ether and Air

Salty (*lavana*):
Fire and Water

Pungent (*katu*):
Fire and Air

SWEET: THE SATTVIC STAPLE

Sweet, comprising earth and water, is found in foods that are heavy, oily, sticky, and cool. These foods nourish and nurture the body and nerves, creating feelings of pleasure, comfort, and love. Think about the gooey, moist nature of the brain and spinal cord as you eat nicely oiled foods. Sweet cravings are sometimes a reflection of a craving for loving energy. The grounding and stabilizing qualities of sweet foods make them the staple of a sattvic diet, for they create an experience of satisfaction and fulfillment. In excess, however, their heavy quality can slow the body down, eventually leading to a state of tamas.

Sweet taste is found in complex carbohydrates, such as whole grains, root vegetables (such as beets, carrots, sweet potatoes, parsnips), nuts and seeds, ripe fruits, dairy products, fresh-pressed oils, sugar cane, and honey, to name a few. Overly sweet foods and processed sugars, such as cake and ice cream, are tamasic and will clog the channels and slow mental functions, leading to lethargy.

Signs of Satisfaction
Relaxation after meals
Sound sleep
Love

Your Taste Buds

— ◆ ◆ ◆ —

Have you ever tried to recreate a restaurant dish, cocktail, or specialty coffee at home? It's shocking how much salt and sugar it takes to achieve a taste that has become habitual through the habit of eating out. It can be very eye-opening to observe the salt or sugar going into a dish you might enjoy often at a restaurant. To enjoy more food at home, give yourself a little time to allow your taste buds to come back to square one. Your own simple cooking will start to taste good, and the outside food will begin to seem intense. Just give it some time, and you will be amazed by how much your palate changes.

SOUR, SALTY, AND PUNGENT: THE RAJASIC RASCALS

I know I called them rascals, but each of these tastes is needed in small amounts. Sour, salty, and pungent tastes are found in foods with hot, sharp, penetrating qualities. These three tastes increase the digestive fire and aid in the breakdown of sweet foods. Think of them as hard-working helpers to the sattvic staple. Because they are potent, smaller amounts will do. What sour, salty, and pungent all have in common is the fire element. Fired-up foods heat the body (helpful in winter) and stimulate the mind and senses. In the right amount, these tastes can help engage the mind, sharpen focus, jog the memory, and clear the head (try strong ginger tea for a food coma). In the event of lethargy, Ayurveda calls on sour, salty, and pungent to get things moving. Too much of a good thing can result in overstimulation, irritation, obsessive cravings (especially for these three tastes), a short attention span, and a relentless focus on the external world. Overdoing these tastes is like putting the pedal to the metal.

Sour taste is found in unripe fruits and most citrus fruits, ferments, sour cream, stinky cheese, and vinegar. Salty taste is found in sea salt, rock salt, seaweed, soy sauce, and foods to which a lot of salt has been added (especially condiments). Pungent taste is found in chilies, onions, garlic, and alcohol. Restaurant food often overuses these flavors, so be aware of this when you eat out.

Signs of Overstimulation
Waking in the middle of the night or early morning
Inability to sit quietly or spend time alone
Attachment to media devices
Overheating

BITTER AND ASTRINGENT: LIGHTEN UP TAMAS TO CREATE CONGRUENCY

Bitter and astringent tastes share the air element, which has expansive qualities similar to those of the mind, where the movements are governed by the air and space elements. Bitter and astringent foods have light, dry qualities. The light quality of bitter and astringent can lift the heavy, dull experience of tamas to put a spring in your step and encourage a spiritual perspective on life. These tastes expand the mind and cleanse the body. Just be careful, as too much expanding and cleansing may make you unstable. Try getting your calories from grapefruits for a few days, and you will see what I mean. Too many bitter and astringent foods will dry out your tissues and can lead to depletion, loss of libido, and lack of enthusiasm. The modern diet often overlooks these tastes and overdoes the others, but overzealous health nuts can display excessive bitter and astringent qualities.

I've included a delicious selection of well-balanced, light dishes to add to your repertoire that will help revitalize and motivate you. Bitter and astringent foods include leafy greens, berries, stone fruits, summer squashes, fresh herbs, and turmeric.

> **Signs of Spiritual Perspective**
> Waking early and feeling refreshed
> Gratitude
> The choice of nourishing relationships and activities
> Smooth decision-making process

DIVING DEEPER: VIRYA AND VIPAKA

In some cases, a food is classified as rajasic, but it doesn't taste salty, sour, or pungent. You don't need to understand all this in depth to eat well, but if a food isn't considered sattvic for everyday use, here's why.

Virya is the effect a food has on the digestive tract after it is swallowed. This can be heating or cooling. Foods that heat the gut can be irritants, increasing hot emotions and excitability in the mind. An example is eggplant, which tastes sweet enough but has a heating virya. Unless heat is indicated, foods of this nature should be used sparingly. You will find these food items on the rajas list.

Vipaka is the effect a food has on the body after it has been digested. This effect can also be either heating or cooling. Vipaka can bring the nourishing, cooling effects of sweet taste; the hot, dry effects of pungent taste; or the hot, moist effects of sour taste. While foods with sweet vipaka are sattvic, pungent and sour vipaka will excite the mind. Ginger, for example, tastes spicy but has the calming effects of sweet vipaka and is a staple spice in sattvic cooking.

the sattvic diet

If I get in the habit of eating heavy meals at night, I have a harder time waking up and getting going in the mornings. After several days, I start to wake feeling sad and lose my zest for the day ahead. Once I learned about the energy of tamas—a heavy, dense sense of inertia that is increased by heavy foods at night—this knowledge illuminated the effects of my daily habits. As I practiced remembering this heavy feeling when tempted by a rich evening meal, the allurement of dinner eventually began to fade. It was a natural and slow progression that I didn't have to fight for.

The knowledge only works if you practice, though. You will see that the energy of sattva is promoted by high-vibration foods; simple, fresh, and organic foods; and *how* you eat (in a hurry versus relaxed). So many of these diet and lifestyle tips will strike you as common sense. The wonder of this "science of life" is that it isn't teaching us anything we don't already know; it is simply pointing to the patterns of nature and how to live in sync. Good food + Good intention = Full prana.

The sattvic diet is an integral part of Ayurveda's grand plan for mental wellness. I'm loath to use that term, because *diet* is an often-misused word that can suggest speedy weight loss, or a newfangled eating system that cures all. What I mean is the sattvic *lifestyle*, of which food is an important part. Lucky for us, cooking is a great entry point to mental balance and well-being. Just adding a few new dishes in your weekly menu, upping your lunch game, and eating less at night are great places to start.

The wisdom of Ayurveda teaches that creating change in the body also affects the mind. It's a win-win!

WHAT ARE SATTVIC FOODS?

"Foods that the sattvic are drawn to promote vitality, health, pleasure, strength, and long life, and are fresh, firm, succulent, and tasty."
—BHAGAVAD GITA

Sattvic foods are whole foods: grains, legumes, fruits, nuts, seeds, fresh dairy, and vegetables. The main principle is to *choose foods that are rich in prana, or life force*. These foods digest well, nourish the tissues, balance the gunas, and cultivate higher mind. Food substances get prana from their environment, like nutritious soil, sunshine, water, and the attentiveness of gardeners and farmers.

TASTES AND MAHA GUNAS

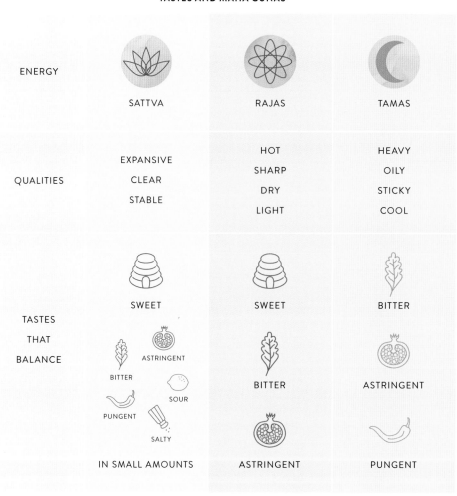

ENERGY	SATTVA	RAJAS	TAMAS
QUALITIES	EXPANSIVE CLEAR STABLE	HOT SHARP DRY LIGHT	HEAVY OILY STICKY COOL
TASTES THAT BALANCE	SWEET BITTER ASTRINGENT PUNGENT SOUR SALTY IN SMALL AMOUNTS	SWEET BITTER ASTRINGENT	BITTER ASTRINGENT PUNGENT

This seems obvious, but modern farming practices denature common foods in various ways along the line from seed to soil, harvest to processing. The trick, these days, is to find what I call "real food." Real food fosters a connection to the natural world around us, whereas processed food eventually causes a disconnect. The foods that carry life force are non-GMO (genetically modified organism); fresh from the farm; and sweet, like apples, melons, carrots, and yams—or whichever fruits and vegetables grow in your climate. This may require acclimating your taste buds to natural flavors and learning how to prepare meals efficiently from unprocessed foods. That is exactly what I mean to do with this book: help you figure out how to make those meals so you will be inspired to eat this way on a daily basis. Both your body and your mind will thank you.

Living in a cold climate, the thing I miss the most is papaya. In India, papayas are bright salmon in color, and they drip red juice as you cut them. They taste like pure nectar. In Boston, papayas are pale and tasteless in comparison. Because they were picked before they were ripe and have traveled far, they have lost their life energy. When a food loses its mojo, it will be stale, limp, and dry. I am one of those ladies you see at the market inspecting all the produce. I enjoy feeling for the vitality and healing potential of the foods that will come home with me.

Foods that are fresh, firm (not wilted or soggy), or succulent (full of naturally occurring moisture, like crisp cucumbers) will obviously be tasty—they are full of life! Like increases like, and fresh foods will make all of their qualities appear in the body: youth, firmness, juiciness, and full of life. Think of how a cucumber gets if it sits a day too long: shriveled, limp, soggy. So if like increases like, you don't want to eat old vegetables. Certain foods that predominate in natural sweet taste, such as root vegetables, rice, and juicy fruits like mango and grapes, are revered for promoting sattva with the nourishing qualities of the earth and water elements (you can find these in the table of sattvic foods on page 66).

In the sattvic diet, eggs, which are quite heating, are not considered vegetarian. Many vegetarians do eat eggs, but in India, "pure veg" means no eggs. Rarely will you find a vegan, as natural dairy is a staple that provides good fats and proteins for those who tolerate it well. Please do not impose dietary restrictions on yourself that feel uncomfortable. Changes in the diet will come as the result of healthy cravings, which arise slowly due to honest observation of what makes you feel good. Moving in the direction of peace and harmony within yourself is a gradual and kind process that is guided from within.

Sattvic

- Organic
- Fresh
- Local
- Seasonal
- Least processed
- Vegetarian

Not Sattvic

- Canned (Home canning, however, is as close to sattvic as you can get in winter.)
- Frozen
- Pickled and fermented (unless it's homemade or local and freshly made in small batches)
- Boxed, premixed, machine-chopped, artificially flavored or colored
- Dry (including finely milled flour goods, crackers, and chips)
- Fried
- Leftover
- Hot and spicy

Finding Real Food

— ♦ ♦ ♦ —

- *Grow your own.* If you have some space, build a raised bed and plant some veggies. If you don't, consider joining a local farm that offers shares of its harvest for an annual fee. Community Supported Agriculture (CSA) keeps small, organic farms in business.
- *Shop the farmers' market.* The longer a food travels, the more prana seeps out. Work a stop at the local farmers' market into your schedule, and hit it when the growing season is on. Find affordable dairy, produce, and homemade wonders. Enjoy the brighter appearance and aroma of fresh food.
- *Shop the perimeter.* In grocery stores, notice how all the bottles and cans are in the aisles, and the dairy, deli, and produce are on the edges. Don't go in the middle unless you know what you're doing there! Condiments are suspect. I'll be suggesting some sattvic standbys for full-bodied flavor.
- *Keep to the seasonal rhythm.* In the warm season, eat what's growing. In the cool season, eat more stored grains, legumes, nuts, seeds, ghee, hearty greens, and sweet potatoes. There are lots of ways to prepare these items in the recipe section!
- *Look for non-GMO.* It is too soon to identify the potential effects of consuming foods previously unknown to nature.

Food Categories	Sattvic
Fruits	Most fresh, ripe fruit: plums, peaches, apples, pears, grapes, berries, cherries, apricots, figs, bananas, melons, pomegranates, raisins, cranberries
Vegetables	Most fresh, seasonal vegetables: fennel, kale, Swiss chard, summer and winter squashes, cabbage, carrots, sweet potatoes and yams, turnips, parsnips, beets, cucumbers, leafy greens, celery
Grains	Rice (brown, red, white basmati), wild rice, quinoa, amaranth, teff, kamut, millet, buckwheat, barley, oats
Beans	Small beans: mung beans, lentils, black beans,* sprouted
Dairy	Nonhomogenized cow's milk, homemade yogurt, goat's milk
Fats	Ghee, coconut oil, coconut meat Raw nuts and seeds: almonds, cashews, pecans, walnuts,* sesame seeds,* hemp seeds, chia seeds, flaxseeds, sunflower seeds
Spices	Turmeric, cardamom, coriander, cumin, fennel, cinnamon, ginger, hing (asafatida, see the glossary)
Extras	Herbal teas (licorice, fennel, ginger)
Sweets	Coconut sugar, maple syrup, raw cane juice, raw honey

*In moderation (one or two times per week)

Choosing foods that are homemade as opposed to processed and preserved, fresh as opposed to fried or soggy, and succulent instead of dried will promote longevity. The more often you choose real food, the better you will feel, but your diet doesn't have to be perfect. The pursuit of perfection in itself creates imbalance in the mind. Remember that a true state of sattva leaves some room for spontaneity and innocent enjoyment without judgment.

Sattvic foods that promote harmony in the mind will reduce the mental activity of rajas and the inertia of tamas. It is that simple, so learning what foods are sattvic and how to prepare them is most important.

RAJASIC FOODS

"Foods that please the rajasic—bitter or salty or sour, hot or harsh
or pungent—cause pain, disease, and discomfort."
—BHAGAVAD GITA

Sour, salty, and pungent foods increase agni (digestive fire), promote circulation, keep the body warm, and aid in the digestion of heavy foods. In excess, they will stimulate, irritate, and inflame. Each of us must discover our own threshold for excess (discomfort, like acid stomach, will point the finger). Those with colder bodies will crave, and need, more of these warming tastes, such as ginger tea. Those who run hot will, in a state of balance, crave the calming, cooling flavors of sweet, bitter, and astringent, such as a green juice.

You will find that some foods categorized as rajasic may not taste sour or pungent, but they have a heating effect on the gut and can cause mental agitations such as irritability or an overactive mind. A state of "discomfort," as the Gita states, is distracting and sometimes overwhelming, and it does not promote harmony in the mind.

	FOODS THAT INCREASE EXCITABILITY IN THE MIND
Foods	**Rajasic**
Fruits	Sour fruits: oranges, lemons (in excess), unripe mango, tamarind, guava Canned fruits | Dried dates
Vegetables	Olives, garlic, onion, white potatoes, bell pepper, eggplant, tomatoes, chilies, spicy radishes, spicy greens and cruciferous vegetables (in excess), pickles
Grains	White flour | Dry grains (in excess): corn, millet, buckwheat
Beans	Large beans: chickpeas, cannellini, kidney beans
Dairy	Eggs, sour cream, cottage cheese, store-bought/sour yogurt, hard or aged cheeses, cream, ice cream
Fats	Pumpkin seeds and avocado (in excess), fried foods
Spices	Salt, vinegar, hot sauce, cayenne, black pepper
Extras	Kombucha, coffee, caffeine, fermented foods (unless homemade), bubbly water, alcohol, packaged snack foods
Sweets	White sugar, brown sugar, molasses

TAMASIC FOODS

"The preferred foods of the tamasic are stale, overcooked, tasteless, contaminated, impure, filthy, putrid, and rotten."
—BHAGAVAD GITA

This is pretty extreme, so let's try to modernize it a bit. Foods that increase the lethargic, stagnant energy of tamas are going to slow you down, gunk up your gut, and tax your body rather than nourish it. Foods that are old and soggy, burned, fried, or filled with chemical flavorings, preservatives, or hydrogenated oils lack prana and will, if eaten regularly, have a dulling effect on your mind and body. This can contribute to brain fog, depression, and a lack of enthusiasm. For example, notice the dull colors and flavors of leftovers versus the vibrant appearance and aroma of freshly cooked food. If you are accustomed to leftovers, it becomes easy not to notice, but with regular consumption of fresh, tasty food and the enjoyment of postdigestive clarity and energy, leftovers lose their appeal.

In a state of stagnation, you will need to enlist a bit of rajas to get things moving. It is hard to go from stagnation to contentment without a bit of action like aerobic exercise.

FOODS THAT INCREASE HEAVINESS IN THE MIND

Foods	Tamasic
Fruits	Fruits that are frozen, overripe, or out of season
Vegetables	Mushrooms, pumpkin (in excess) Vegetables that are frozen, GMO, wilted, or out of season
Grains	Wheat
Beans	Isolated soy protein
Dairy	All cheeses, eggs, processed milk, cold milk, ice cream
Fats	Margarines, canola oil, lard, peanuts, rancid fats (old, or vegetable and nut oils cooked at high heat), roasted nuts, packaged pastries
Spices	Monosodium glutamate (MSG)
Extras	Meat, fish, fried foods, fast foods, leftovers, microwaved foods, drugs and alcohol, potato chips
Sweets	White sugar, soft drinks, artificial sweeteners, cooked honey

FOOD GROUPS

Ayurveda tells us that a food's nature can be altered by its processing. For instance, the quality of a wheat berry, and its effect on the system, is quite different after it has been milled to a flour, and even more so if it has been bleached. As another example, the gassy quality of beans can be reduced by soaking. So, a bean or a wheat berry can have different effects based on the form in which it is served and the cooking process. These are general guidelines for creating the most beneficial foods with the common staples of a modern diet.

Grains. Non-GMO, "ancient," and heirloom varieties of grains will be closer to natural than large-scale farmed grains. To serve "succulent" grains, as recommended by the Bhagavad Gita, be sure to cook them until they are soft, and don't skimp on the water. Fluff with a fork before serving to create pleasing, light whole grains.

Beans. The name of the game is to eat small beans, such as mung and lentil, which are easier to digest. They soften and moisten quickly and more completely through the cooking process. Large beans, such as garbanzo and kidney, eaten in excess, can fill the digestive tract with air, which is aggravating and irritating to the body—and therefore the mind. Some people can eat beans with no problem, others have to moderate even small beans. Always soak them overnight, and cook them well with some spices and fat to balance their light, dry qualities.

Dairy. The milk of ancient times was a different substance than what is widely available today. Raw milk, if available, is the closest thing to small-batch milk, fresh from the family cow. Modern milk is homogenized and pasteurized. While Ayurveda has always recommended boiling raw milk before consuming it, large-scale pasteurization kills some of the enzymes in milk, which can make it harder to digest.

A Middle Road on Leftovers

— ◆ ◆ ◆ —

I see a lot of people who get anxious about not eating leftovers. The well-oiled machine of a working family kitchen may require meals being served again as lunches or warmed up a day or two after the fact. A rule of thumb: try to cook simple every other day and have just one day of leftovers. You and yours will notice the difference.

Homogenization alters the structure of fat molecules in milk so they stay suspended rather than separating, as in cream-top milks. While traditional Ayurveda describes separating the fat from milk (see the recipe for Lassi on page 204) and using it in specific ways for health benefits, the modern process of homogenization can render fat molecules difficult to digest and more likely to clog the subtle channels of the body and create ama. Both of these results lead to tamas. If you can't get farm-fresh raw milk (illegal in some states!), buy organic, grass-fed, nonhomogenized milk, which is now becoming available in grocery stores. If you still don't digest milk well, you will find dairy-free alternatives in most of the recipes.

Meat. All meat is considered tamasic because it is, well, dead. You can't get more lethargic than that. The larger and slower the animal, the more tamas its meat will impart (cows are number one). In addition, meat is acid-forming and heavy, which promotes both rajas and tamas. The meat of animals and fish is used medicinally in cases of deficiency but is otherwise avoided.

Fats. Bad fats, I'm convinced by my own experience, are the worst thing for the body. Not only do indigestible fats make the body fat, but they clog the channels, block the movements of prana, and cloud the mind. Fats are "bad" when they don't digest, and that happens when oils are rancid or when a meal contains more fat than the body can break down at the time. Fried food is never indicated. Low-quality and packaged baked goods are also suspect. When cooking, favor heat-tolerant oils like coconut and ghee. Canola, olive, and large-scale vegetable oils are suspect. It is very important to buy organic cultured butter and small-batch oils—from your own country if possible to cut down on travel time—and to make your own ghee.

Nuts and Seeds. Roasting nuts will change their effects on the body by aging their oils. Take care to keep fresh nuts and seeds refrigerated, and roast them fresh at home. Most nuts are slightly heating and best eaten in moderation, except for almonds, which are revered for being cooling and moist in their raw form after soaking. As a rule of thumb, seeds such as hemp, sunflower, and flax are lighter than nuts and easier to break down.

Vegetables. Cooking vegetables renders them soft, moist, and smooth—all calming qualities. Fermenting and pickling locally, in small batches, can be an excellent digestive aid in the right amount and in cooler weather. A handful of vegetable varieties, especially tomatoes, will have a heating effect on the body, increasing reactivity in the mind when used daily. Choose local, vibrant, succulent vegetables, and avoid wilted or discolored specimens.

Fruits. Most fruits, when in season and ripe, will have a nourishing, satisfying effect on your mind and body. Notice how fruits bought out of season or outside their natural climates never become fully ripe and sweet. Some fruits, like citrus, can have a sour postdigestive effect, heat the body, and overstimulate the mind when used daily.

Spices. Fresh is best! If a spice is in its whole form, it is considered potent up to one year. After grinding, it is good for up to three months. Buy spices in bulk, in amounts you can use up easily.

Fresh herbs are amazing for flavoring food and are easy to grow. The cooling herbs mint and cilantro are prized in the sattvic diet.

Food Is Love

◆ ◆ ◆

Intention and attitude are key aspects to the process of digestion and the actions foods make in the body and mind. Simply choosing foods with joy and overall satisfaction in mind, rather than anxiety about "doing it right," is the way to go. Food is love, and if treated as such, it will nourish you on every level.

OAT GROATS

OATS

MILLET

QUINOA

BULGUR
WHEAT

BASMATI
RICE

WILD RICE

BUCKWHEAT

BROWN
BASMATI
RICE

GREEN
MUNG
BEANS

SPLIT YELLOW
MUNG BEANS

CHICKPEAS

FRENCH
LENTILS

RED
LENTILS

GREEN
LENTILS

CINNAMON STICKS

TURMERIC

PINK SALT

STAR ANISE

AJWAIN

SESAME SEEDS

CLOVES

CARDAMOM PODS

FRESH GINGER

HING/ ASAFETIDA

FENNEL SEEDS

CUMIN SEEDS

MUSTARD SEEDS

FENUGREEK

CORIANDER SEEDS

HOW TO EAT SATTVIC

How you eat is every bit as important as *what* you eat. Preparing and eating meals with satisfaction in mind and in accordance with healthy digestive practices will give you the best results.

Ahara rasa, the nutritive liquid resulting from food being broken down in the stomach, is the building block of a balanced body. If your digestion is not working properly, it can lead to imbalances. Incomplete digestion can result from eating too fast, eating when you're not hungry, or eating heavy foods at night. The following practices can increase digestive power and a feeling of satisfaction after meals.

Slow down. As mealtime approaches, begin checking in with your body. What does the hunger feel like? Are any qualities at the forefront, such as heat or cold, dryness in your mouth, nose, or skin? Are any emotions coming through, such as irritation, sadness, or anxiety? Simply pay attention and take note, without any judgment, to what is going on in this moment. This action of bringing the attention into your body and away from the work of the morning or afternoon encourages discernment, leading to better meal choices and an easier time of implementing the practices that follow.

Sit down. Sitting down while eating is as important for the digestive organs as it is for the mind. The organs relax and prepare to do their jobs when you sit. Take three deep breaths, focus on the activity at hand, and give thanks for the food before beginning.

Quiet down. Talking sends energy out of your mouth while the food is going in. Eating quietly will ensure that the downward-moving energy of chewing, swallowing, and digesting cruises along down the line. Avoid scheduling meetings and phone calls, watching TV, or reading during mealtimes.

Eat more fats and proteins at lunch and a lighter meal at night. Taking the time to focus on solid nutrition at midday ensures that your body is properly fueled and food is fully digested throughout the afternoon. Not eating enough can lead to relying on stimulants or adrenaline until dinner, increasing rajas in the mind. Then eating slowly to digest foods at night (cheese, white bread, fries, meat) increases tamas in the mind by increasing the heavy quality. This vicious cycle can be headed off at lunchtime. *Note:* Those who get up early, especially those who exercise early, may find breakfast to be an important meal as well.

Eat only when hungry. This can take some practice, but it is number one in preserving a strong digestive fire. The habit of eating to fuel an overactive mind is very common. Just begin by pausing before a snack to tune in to your stomach—is there hunger? Even better, tune in and wait ten minutes before snacking. It is likely the compulsion to eat will subside. It is common for this desire to come in the evening as well, when the mind is still hyperactive from the day. The body wants to increase tamas, slow down, and rest, so it makes sense that the body would crave heavy qualities from comfort foods at the end of the day to stabilize and replenish. A sattvic sensibility, however, will look first toward rejuvenating activities when the appetite is dull, replenishing energy without taxing the gut.

Have consistent mealtimes. The whole system, mind and body, responds well to routine. Consistent mealtimes train the digestive juices to show up, ready to rock, at the appropriate times, and the mind relaxes into the routine, free of wondering when and what the next meal will be. Regular mealtimes build trust between mind and body by showing the body that attention is being directed toward proper nourishment. Think of how discombobulated dogs get when their usual mealtimes are changed. On a subtle level, that can happen to us too.

Eat light, or not at all, when angry or anxious. The Ayurveda texts list states of mind that are not ideal for digestion. Two biggies, worry and anger, are prevalent emotions for many. At times when the mind is occupied with such turbulence, nothing will digest well, and it is best to take warm liquids and wait until things calm down to eat.

Drink warm or room temperature water. Keep that cozy feeling going in your gut by avoiding cold drinks and favoring warm water. Warm water does wonders to rehydrate and calm the body.

Eat seasonal and local. Increase prana by enjoying fresh foods that have had minimal processing and that haven't traveled far. Seasonal foods offer the qualities necessary to balance the current environment. If it's cold out, cook your food.

Ahara: Traditional Guidelines for Healthy Digestion

——— ◆◆◆ ———

To enjoy digestion that is free of gas, bloating, acid stomach, or inflammation, do your best to observe the following.

- Do not take iced drinks, especially with meals. Ask for plain water at restaurants.
- Drink warm water, and carry a thermos instead of a water bottle—especially when it's cold out!
- Favor warm, cooked foods, and reduce leftovers.
- Wait two hours after meals before drinking much.
- Space out your meals, probably by at least three to four hours, to allow for complete digestion before eating again. Avoid grazing; your digestive fire can never keep up with constant input.
- Take your time when eating, and take a little rest for ten minutes after, but do not sleep after eating.
- Take a relaxing walk after eating.
- If you are going to have a treat, have it with lunch, when your digestion is strongest, and do not eat again until dinner.
- Do not mix meat and fish with milk, as all three are difficult to digest and, in combination, can result in ama, or toxicity.
- Avoid mixing raw fruits, especially melons and bananas, with cow's milk products. This can cause a sour stomach and gas. The warming, sweet nature of dates, however, combines well with milk.

5

the
sattvic lifestyle

HOW TO BEAUTIFY YOUR EXTERNAL
AND INTERNAL WORLDS

CLASSICAL AYURVEDA TEXTS SPEAK a good deal about "pleasing the senses." Back in the day, this was achieved by wearing fresh flowers in the hair; making floral garlands for the home and temple daily; enjoying good company; and eating fresh, fragrant foods and spices. This chapter will suggest a number of ways to promote beauty in your kitchen, home, and workspace. A balanced mind can be supported from the inside out, as well as from the outside in. Consider the difference in how you feel walking into a cluttered office versus a tidy one, a dirty kitchen versus a sparkling one. Setting the stage for relaxation and productivity, you can calm your mind through the type of energies with which you surround yourself. Color, texture, sound, aroma, and intention gently (or not so gently) guide the mind to a certain experience, before the work or cooking has even begun. A natural, pleasant environment promotes a natural, pleasant state of mind.

For some of us, working from the outside in is a simpler place to start on the path toward promoting balance, while for others, it may be the other way around. This chapter contains theories and practices to help with both. The external life tends to be easier to modify, as it is more tangible. The results of cleaning the kitchen or leaving a big mess are often easy to recognize. Purifying the mind of its habitual patterns is subtle and requires a keen inner eye. For most of us, that kind of sight is carefully cultivated. As the mind is purified, the inherent beauty of the inner world shines forth. For the beginner to Ayurvedic living, simply organizing and beautifying the kitchen is an anchoring practice. Go ahead, read on, and if something jumps out at you, that's a good place to start. And remember—eating a primarily sattvic diet makes purifying inside and out easier, so hit up those recipes too.

your external world: cultivating sattva in your home and workspace

The Sanskrit word *sukha* means "happiness, good space." Ayurveda works by promoting "good space" in the internal and external worlds—your body, mind, and environment. Whether you are raising a family or living alone, taking a little time to create natural beauty in your living space encourages positive vibrations in the mind. It is not about doing major redecorating, but simply turning your attention to inspiring sights, smells, sounds, tastes, and activities. While it can seem like just another chore to follow these suggestions, think of them as setting intentions for your overall peace of mind.

A little TLC spent on your home slowly changes the landscape of the mind. Transformation is twofold: (1) you make your environment a wonderful place to be, and (2) by taking pleasure in the beautification of your environment, you create good space within. This might require a shift in the way you view housework. We all have to do the cleaning and tidying anyhow, so why not see it as an opportunity to create beauty? I catch myself getting fed up with washing dishes all the time, so dishes are a prime opportunity for me to practice sukha. *Sometimes*, I can relax and enjoy it! Start with something that sounds doable rather than your least favorite chore.

KITCHEN

Spend some quality time sprucing things up to make your kitchen inviting—somewhere you'd like to be. Try these suggestions to encourage sattva:

- *Flowers and living plants:* Keep a flowering plant or fresh flowers in your kitchen. Snipping the ends and changing flowers' water daily preserves their freshness.
- *Colors:* Simple, natural colors—especially white, blue, yellow, and pastels—increase sattva. Crazy paint jobs in the kitchen do not encourage a relaxing experience.
- *Materials:* Avoid plastic accessories, and choose products made from natural materials when you can. Use bamboo and wooden serving and stirring utensils and cutting boards, stainless steel pots, and cast-iron pots and pans. Replace paper towels with washable kitchen towels, and use natural sponges.
- *Cleaning products:* Use a natural cleaner to wipe down counters and visible surfaces. Bonus tips: Vinegar works well for ants, and adding a few drops of eucalyptus, lemon, or balsam oil to your cleanser makes thing smell fresh.

THE SATTVIC LIFESTYLE

PANTRY

This is one place where getting the appropriate "gear" will really help create a calming space. Collecting glass nut-butter jars or buying a case of canning jars will provide a uniform look in the cabinet for stacking and storing dry goods. Keep nuts, seeds, grains, and legumes in glass jars. I prefer the sixteen-ounce or larger variety because they hold a good amount and allow you to buy fresh as needed.

Avoid buying huge quantities and hanging on to dry goods for more than a year, as they will lose their prana. Keep spices in glass jars as well, and buy them fresh in bulk at a store with a good turnover. An Indian "spice box" is the traditional way to store culinary spices; it includes seven small cups and allows the cook to have the full palate within reach. Avoid keeping things in plastic bags that pile up and get old.

The pantry needs to be refreshed every season. Be sure to go through it when the weather shifts and pull the appropriate items to the front so you can eat with the seasons.

AT THE TABLE

Whether you are setting your table for ten people or just yourself, a beautiful table setting is equally important. Often people tell me they can't get excited about cooking for one, so they let it slide. You are cooking for the universe! We have all heard the saying "Your body is a temple"; that means it is a vehicle for doing good work and deserves your love and respect. Taking time to sit down and enjoy the process is often missing at mealtimes, and your digestion suffers. The practice of sitting down while eating is key to good digestive health, and having a nice place to sit down supports a peaceful mealtime.

Make sure you like the shapes and textures of your dishware. For example, I like local pottery; I'm a huge fan of wide bowls, not deep ones; and I think sporks and spoons with long handles are fun. Try using a set of cloth napkins and a few matching placemats. Keep a plant or fresh flowers on the table, and have the table by a sunlit window if you can—it is wonderful to meditate on nature while eating. I also recommend having comfortable chairs that encourage good posture. I find chairs with armrests helpful because they make me sit back and relax between bites, rather than putting my elbows on the table and hunching over. Try to plate your food at the stove and move over to the sit-down table to begin eating, or arrange everything on the table and then sit down and begin.

In the event that buying new products or overhauling the kitchen is not in your budget, keep in mind that intention and attitude are the most effective changes you can make. Furniture for dining can be invented creatively, such as a low table and cushions or simply moving a desk chair over to the living room table. Sprucing things up with a happy houseplant does not have to be expensive and just requires attention and water.

On the go? Invest in a waterproof lunch bag that fits into your work/travel bag and a sealable container or stainless steel thermos for the food (lots of natural container options are available these days if you look in natural foods markets). Add in a set of bamboo or wooden utensils and a cloth napkin, and you'll always be prepared for a nourishing, gourmet moment.

BATHROOM

Modern Ayurveda recommends not putting anything on your body that you wouldn't put in your mouth. A lot of questionable chemicals show up in the bathroom—in cleaners, soaps, and cosmetics. Chemicals are foreign to the body, and their effects on bodies and brains can be disruptive and incredibly detrimental.

To enjoy optimal health and wellness, try to phase these out in favor of natural options:

Bleach: Try natural disinfectants.

Soap: Try a simple castile soap that can do it all. Simply refill dispensers at the sink and shower. Natural bar soaps with Ayurvedic herbs for different skin types are also available at most health food stores.

Makeup and hair: There are more natural options coming on the market all the time. Look for sulfate-free products, and be sure to read the ingredients list. With makeup, look for natural ingredients, and switch out most items every six months to avoid bacteria. Makeup can be fun, but don't forget that the true-you is already beautiful without it. A healthy diet is the best cosmetic, and with more focus on what goes *in* your body, what goes *on* your body will naturally shift as well. For example, coconut oil is an excellent facial moisturizer for many skin types, and deodorant can be replaced by a sattvic diet (which doesn't make BO) in most cases. (See appendix 1 for more details on natural body care.)

Bathing: Beautify your body by doing self-massage regularly. (You will find information about how to incorporate this into your routine and what oils to use in appendix 1.) The ancient texts say that oil massage is the best longevity practice and makes the body strong and immune to diseases.

On a budget? *Use less stuff.* We live in a culture where many unnecessary products are touted to relieve the insecurities planted by the same touts. The body is viewed as something that needs to be altered, as though there is something wrong with eyebrows and armpits. Consider that health and beauty really result from an experience of balance in mind and body.

WORKSPACE

Whether you work from home, in a truck, or in a cubicle, putting a little soul into your workspace keeps things from getting stagnant or too messy. There needs to be something in the space to remind you of your heart. Keep pictures of loved ones or beautiful places to which you connect, and try to bring in natural items like seasonal acorns, pinecones, clovers, or blossoms.

I had a client who was suffering in an aggressive work environment and was losing her sense of self. I recommended that she bring sweet-smelling flowers to her desk to remind her of her own inherent beauty and sweetness. She opted instead to bring in a gaudy seasonal decoration that made her smile and keep her sense of humor! Not everybody is into flowers, so whatever reminds you of your true self is a great addition to your workspace.

your internal world: purifying the mind

Your internal world is essentially a good space. Ayurveda tells us a root cause of mental imbalance is identifying with psychological stress rather than cosmic consciousness. We forget what is real. Imagine waking up every day thinking, "I am a part of the circle of life," versus, "I have so much to do today." Imagine if, when you drove on the highway, billboards showed pictures of gorgeous natural beauty with reminders like, "Enjoy the journey," rather than ads for car insurance and a reminder that you might get rear-ended. Stress is reinforced by the pace and focus of modern life. When the good space of pure consciousness is occupied by stress, it's easy to forget what good feels like. Purification of the internal world is a slow reprogramming process of steadily introducing the qualities of simplicity and interconnection. In time, the mind recognizes what is real more often.

These rewards do not come in a matter of days or even weeks, but once the experience of clarity in the mind is established, *even some of the time*, it becomes familiar and easier to come back to. The good news is that Yoga and Ayurveda have provided us with a road map for this journey.

The sensory faculties, or indriyas, are the windows into our internal world. Indriyas include the eyes, ears, nose, tongue, and skin. They have two parts: the physical organ of each sense, and the *energy* enlivening each sense. The organs themselves cannot function without prana. When we watch TV or listen to music, for example, our attention goes out through the eyes and ears to connect to sights and sounds, and the brain and nervous system then digests what is seen and heard. Watching TV actually requires our energy! When we are always watching or listening to something, never enjoying a little peace and quiet, prana is always going *out*. In this state of imbalance, the internal world does not receive enough energy. Ayurvedic remedies for this state include consciously directing prana inward through breathing, yoga postures, meditation, and visualization.

TAKING CARE OF YOUR SENSES

With long-term imbalance, the sense organs themselves become overworked and begin to break down. The senses slowly become dull, like the smoker who needs to put tons of salt on everything, the drummer who doesn't wear earplugs and can't hear offstage, or the computer programmer whose vision blurs toward the end of the day. The organs themselves begin to malfunction or break down, and hearing aids or glasses are used to extend their life. A little bit of care along the way supports longevity of these organs and their functions. Here are a few general suggestions to reduce strain on the sense organs.

Pratyahara: Training the Attention

——— ◆ ◆ ◆ ———

Imagine you are trying to pay attention to a book, and your neighbor is blasting music or cooking chili peppers that burn your nose. Paying attention will be increasingly difficult as you become distracted by the sound or smell. With practice, you can focus your attention, but the untrained energy of the sense organs is quite disorderly, especially with stimulation everywhere. The organs can't help it, they are hardwired to gather information that then needs to be processed by the mind. It takes devoted practice, but *pratyahara* (the yogic discipline of withdrawing the sense organs) trains students to notice and moderate the movements of the senses. The next time you are in a yoga class, notice when you are looking at other people or out the window, and bring your eyes back to a point on your own body. With guidance and time, you can train your senses to settle down and react less to the stimuli around you. With this skill, you can reduce your overall stress.

Hearing. Avoid wearing headphones when you are out, and when you can, reduce the amount of time spent chatting on the phone, in favor of quiet.

Sight. Limit computer, smartphone, and TV time as much as possible. Get specific, and notice how many minutes per day feels appropriate. Rest your eyes by closing them and taking a few deep breaths from time to time. If this proves difficult, try lying down with an eye pillow over your eyes to block out the light for a few minutes.

Taste. Stick to natural, less refined foods without added flavors, white sugars, or too much salt. Acclimate your taste buds to the gentle sensations of natural foods. Practice right speech; notice how much you talk from day to day and whether you tend to criticize or gossip. With a little practice, being quiet becomes calming.

Touch. Oil your skin daily to quiet the nerve endings (see page 301). Favor natural oils, such as sesame, sunflower, coconut, and almond, over conventional moisturizers. Dress warmly when needed. Hug your loved ones.

Smell. Use fewer products containing chemical "fragrance." If you want to use scents, stick to fresh flowers and a light use of essential oils. You will find that a sattvic diet makes you smell good from the inside out.

Moderating Media

——— ◆◆◆ ———

It is not necessary to be available to everybody all the time. Productivity is not the only aim of this life. Turn off the phone and computer sometimes, and enjoy the quiet pleasures your senses can take in as you bring your awareness to the slant of light, the colors of the world around you, a sip of herbal tea. Get outside, shift your attention away from the internal chatter of the mind, and observe the larger world.

STRESS REDUCTION

A deep part of the psyche is hardwired, for old-school survival, to be on orange alert. Even small stressors begin to trigger this survival instinct when the nervous system is overwhelmed. You can practice the suggestions in this section regularly to keep overall stress levels from reaching that orange alert status.

While it's natural to get overwhelmed by suggestions for major changes in life habits, a sense of balance will be elusive until we learn to shift our attention from a to-do list or broken record of stressors to the strong, centered self who says, "I can do this." Keep in mind that long-term stress, which is quite common, is a state of imbalance. Cravings in this state will reflect the imbalance. For example, a desire to keep working or eating even when there is a small voice saying, "Give me a break," is a sign of the disconnect. Shifting from old patterns takes practice, and the path begins with wanting to change. Stop moving, take a breath, close your eyes, and call on your deepest self to override imbalanced cravings and habits. Once natural intelligence shifts the course a bit, it gets easier. It takes repeated effort, and sometimes it's two steps forward, one step back, but change is inevitable. Look over the following suggestions to relieve stress, and maybe one or two will stand out. Start there.

Sleep. According to the Ashtanga Hrdayam, "happiness and unhappiness . . . knowledge and ignorance, life and death—all are dependent on sleep." The right amount of sleep, at the right time of day, ensures a harmonious state of mind. Staying awake at night (much past 10 or 11 P.M.), sleeping in the daytime (except in cases of anxiety, overstimulation, or illness), and sleeping too much or too little are all causes of imbalance. A sleep rhythm for optimal, balanced energy would include bedtime by 10 P.M. and a 6 A.M. wake-up call, give or take. Not everybody needs the same amount of sleep, however, and not every person has the freedom to enjoy the ideal sleep schedule. Anytime you can slow down earlier and enjoy a deep rest, do it. Take a look at what keeps you up; if it's procrastination, surfing the net, or TV, there is room for a change. What I notice is how many people do not give themselves permission to sleep or habitually shove the importance of sleep to the back burner.

> **PRACTICE TIP:** To shift your sleep schedule, change your bedtime and/or wake-up time by fifteen minutes every two weeks until you hit your stride. Do not change to the next fifteen-minute increment if you are still struggling after two weeks. Give it another week or until you feel ready. Stay committed.

Finding a Balance of Work and Relaxation. The heart of imbalance here is a cultural norm we all buy into that tells us work is the important thing. Consider the phrase "Take time for yourself." *Take* it? Who said time for the self should not be an ingrained aspect of daily life? That is where, culturally, we are going wrong and getting into trouble with increased stress levels. How about, "Expect time for yourself." Wouldn't that be a completely different paradigm? No need to feel bad while enjoying an oil massage or a bit of quiet yoga time—hey, everybody's doing it!

Unfortunately, everybody is not doing it, and it begins to feel like moving mountains or being selfish to seek relaxation. While there may truly be a lack of time, I am suggesting the root cause of work imbalance is in the beliefs we hold about work and its paramount importance. If your underlying belief begins to shift, your schedule will as well, even if it seems impossible at the moment.

> **PRACTICE TIP:** As I get busier, I've started noticing when I am giving myself a hard time about relaxing, such as lying on the floor, devouring a novel, or socializing. I really have to focus sometimes on simply feeling OK about "taking" free time, because there is always more to do. I fill this free time with silence, friends, a luxurious oil massage, or restorative yoga/lying around.

Play. Having fun is one of the best things you can do for your overall health. With all this talk about paying attention and focusing the mind, remember that the mind will naturally expand and broaden its horizons through free-form play. Getting outside makes it easy— running around, laughing, and appreciating natural beauty. Go apple picking or hiking, play with pets, and connect with houseplants on a regular basis.

> **PRACTICE TIP:** Notice when you put playtime aside because you are "too busy." Nip this tendency in the bud, and make a date for play as soon as possible. Even a twenty-minute walk outside at lunch can be playful. I like to talk to squirrels.

Meditation and Yoga. Traditionally, a sattvic diet is meant to support the practice of yoga and meditation. It is not necessary to perform elaborate physical feats or austerities to benefit from yoga. A beginning practice of gentle postures can build a relationship between mind and body, teaching you how to listen to what your body needs. Eventually, the practice of concentration and meditation can help you listen to the mind and get to know what is happening in there, get to know the true self as something separate from all that noise. As the mental plane becomes clear, daily life, big choices, and close relationships gain clarity, and you begin to feel closer to your true self more of the time. It is best to undertake the practices of yoga and meditation with an experienced teacher.

PRACTICE TIP: A beginning practice of concentration technique, such as counting ten breaths without losing focus, can begin to train the mind and quiet the senses. (Don't feel bad if you can't do it. Most people can't make it past three in the beginning.)

Community. Environment plays a role in the movements of the maha gunas. Whenever possible, spending time in places that are beautiful to you and with people who lift your spirits will cultivate the higher mind. Take time to notice how you feel after activities and social times, and keep moving toward the ones that leave you feeling balanced and nourished.

> **PRACTICE TIP:** Consider the types of restaurants and stores you frequent. Shopping and eating at locally owned places that source their goods conscientiously will promote sattva. When you are on a budget, simply try eating out less and having more homemade meals, as well as meeting up with friends for potluck meals. Dining in and inviting others to share what you've made spreads positivity.

Seasonal Cleansing. Ayurveda recommends seasonal cleansing as a way to manage the effects a changing environment can have on your health. A simplified diet at the change of seasons allows the body to expel any excessive qualities that may have accumulated during the past season, such as heat from the summer or mucus from the winter. Getting rid of stuff is something the body is good at, as long as you provide a bit of space. A simple diet and rest allows for just that. The annual rhythm of seasonal cleansing supports strong immune and digestive systems. You will find more information on seasonal cleanses in *The Everyday Ayurveda Cookbook: A Seasonal Guide to Eating and Living Well.*

The mind also needs a rest from input and a chance to get rid of stuff. A "cleanse" doesn't have to be about food. Remember, the mind has to digest sensory input, experience, and emotion. When life gets busy, the mind gets overstimulated, and we can experience a backlog of mental "food." A little quiet time, self-care, and a clear desire to relax the mind are necessary to open up some space for mental digestion. Consider how busy the digital world of phones and computers can be, and plan a media break. Cleansing your external space can help too. You can promote mental space by cleaning out your car, closet, or cabinets; or stepping back to take stock of habits that no longer serve you.

The point is to observe an annual rhythm: cleanse at a time of year that works for you for a reset, clean out, or retreat. Without this intention, it's very easy to get swept up in the current of a busy life and forget self-care. (For a three-day mind-cleanse program, see appendix 2.)

This is a lot of suggestions. Give yourself a pat on the back if you start by trying just one.

Five Ways to Cleanse Your Mind

—— ◆ ◆ ◆ ——

Try one of these suggestions for a day of mind cleansing. Find one you like, and consider doing it once a week to support mental balance.

- *Unplug.* Take an entire day off from technology: e-mail, phone, computer, and TV.
- *Power down.* Turn off all screens before dinner, and leave them off for the night.
- *Have an oil massage day.* Carve out time in the morning or evening, and on an empty stomach, begin by oiling your head. Follow by oiling your entire body (described in appendix 1 on page 301). Leave the oil on for thirty to forty-five minutes, then have a hot shower.
- *Enjoy a silent morning.* No phone, radio, TV, or talking until you officially begin your workday.
- *Schedule a play day.* Do only things you want to do, and enjoy doing, all day.

a day in the life:
daily guidelines for a balanced mind

Please don't be overwhelmed by these daily guidelines. Healing your mind is not about perfection—it's about self-awareness. Investigating your own process from balance to imbalance and vice versa, or recognizing the daily triggers that feed overstimulation or cloudiness in the mind, are great places to start. I'm guessing something from this list will jump out at you. Take an honest look at the patterns of your life surrounding particular habits.

A daily rhythm is a matrix of interwoven activities. When you begin to work earnestly at modifying habits in both your internal and external worlds, you will notice how any change creates a ripple effect. The journey toward a strong, healthy mind starts with one change, preferably a simple one, that will undoubtedly illuminate the next step when the time is right.

Expand the mind upon waking. Resist checking e-mail or diving into work first thing in the morning. Allow your mind to expand into the natural environment when you get up. Look out at the sky, notice the elements prevalent in this day; connect to the larger world.

Poop in the morning. Clear bowels equal a clear mind. Give yourself a little quiet time and a cup of hot water, perhaps with lemon. Leave some space for sound bodily function to occur. Do not leave all your chores until the morning, press the snooze alarm, then run around like a crazy person to get of the house. Snoozing is wasted time—that ten minutes could be the difference between stress and comfort at the beginning of the day.

Bathe in the morning. Your body detoxifies during sleep. Bathing in the morning gets rid of toxins and allows you to begin with a clean slate.

Plan your meals. Prepare for success at night by soaking a grain for the next day's hot cereal or prepping veggies for lunch. Skipping meals when you are hungry can create instability in the mind.

Eat lunch. Ground and nourish yourself at midday when the digestive fire is strongest, and you will burn the food as fuel for the rest of the day. Eating too much at night increases tamas, weight gain, and brain fog.

Be tidy. Get in the habit of putting things away soon after you use them, and make sure there is a place for everything. Avoid buying more than you have room for.

Avoid overscheduling. Sometimes self-esteem can hinge on how busy we believe ourselves to be or how involved we are in professional or social circles. You can go crazy trying to keep up with external indicators of self-worth. Keep an eye on the tendency to try to do everything or be a part of everything. Leave some space and time on the calendar for *you*.

Take a mind break at midafternoon. The late afternoon is an important time for harnessing the creativity of space and air elements. Make space by getting outside for a short walk, lying on the floor with your legs up the wall, or even pausing for three minutes of conscious breathing. Pausing the activity of the mind for a few minutes allows space and air to expand, refreshing and rejuvenating the mind. You will find this to be a great replacement for a snack habit. Eating snacks changes the energy in the same way a mind break does. It is often not hunger that fuels the snacking, but a need to shift the energy. You may begin to notice it is when you are overtired that you crave more food.

Quiet your senses in the evening. Activities that allow the senses to rest in the evening are ideal. After dinner, keep it mellow to ensure good sleep and refreshment for tomorrow. Think of TV, excessive talking, or stimulating music as a treat, not daily evening fare. Relax with loved ones, listen to a guided meditation, take a walk outside, or indulge in a computer-free hobby (such as oil massage or stretching) to settle the energy of the day.

Turn off the phone. Do not look at backlit screens after 9 P.M., as this will keep you up late and disturb your sleep.

Lifestyle changes take time and are most successful in increments. With these Ayurvedic suggestions for wellness, I'm giving you a broad overview of how sattvavajaya works, the psychological underpinnings of imbalance and mental patterning, and the healing that is possible with consistent, compassionate focus.

The best news is that Ayurveda's healing strategy of synergizing mind, body, and spirit can happen through lifestyle or diet—but ideally, a little bit of both. For some it's easier to change the diet first, because it is tangible and tasty, and it makes you feel good right away. Sattvic cooking is simple, and I think you'll find the principles pretty easy to incorporate, once you set your mind to it.

PART TWO

THE
SATTVIC
KITCHEN

6

cooking
for
clarity

HEALING YOUR MIND WITH FOOD

THE FOOD YOU EAT can change your state of mind. What a concept! We all have to eat, so why not make it medicinal? The food you eat every day is introducing qualities into both your mind and your body. For example, cheese is heavy, and honey is light—if you eat too much cheese when you were feeling heavy to begin with, your head might end up feeling a little slow and foggy. If you go for homemade, flourless honey-almond bites instead, you will still feel satisfied, while staying bright and sharp. Healing happens through noticing how you are feeling when you eat and making the appropriate choices.

how to use the recipe sections

All of the recipes in this book represent a sattvic diet. This means they are meat-free, egg-free, garlic- and onion-free, and white-sugar-free. Excessively sour, spicy, or denatured foods are not featured in any of the recipes. Chapter 7 teaches you how to prepare a few staples to replace those that are often prepackaged, such as nut milks, flours, and yogurt. It may take some time to notice the difference, as balance doesn't happen overnight. The longer an imbalance has been around, the longer it will take your body/mind to come back to center. Eventually you will get there, so be patient and stay focused on the goal of health and happiness.

RECIPES TO CULTIVATE CONTENTMENT

Chapter 8 showcases sattvic cooking. Recipes focus on naturally balanced tastes and colors of whole foods such as legumes, grains, ripe fruits, and fresh vegetables. All of the flavors and aromatic spices used balance warming with cooling and create dishes delicate enough to keep a clear mind but tasty enough to satisfy. To make it easy for cooks to enjoy fresh food daily and reduce leftovers, recipes have generally smaller yields and are very simple to prepare, except for a few special occasion dishes. This collection of meals, drinks, and treats showcases foods from all seasons, and when a recipe is ideal for certain weather, this is noted. Foods from this chapter will ground and stabilize the body and mind, promoting sustained energy and mental clarity.

RECIPES TO CALM THE MIND

Foods known to cool down and rejuvenate the body help reduce rajas, or restless energy, and result in a calmer mood. Foods that are predominantly sour, salty, and pungent can stimulate the mind and overheat the body. The recipes in chapter 9 call on slightly sweet, cooling foods like almonds, coconut, and grapes to balance an internal environment that may be too fiery. Spices such as coriander, mint, and turmeric contain concentrated amounts of these cooling qualities, and the recipes provide exciting flavors without creating imbalance. As a stimulated mind may crave foods that perpetuate motion, I have tried to create alternatives to satisfy cravings for stimulating foods such as coffee (see Dandi Latte on page 248) and sugary stuff (see Bombay Carrot Halwa on page 245). When feeling overworked, irritated, or edgy, use the recipes in this chapter to slow down, keep cool, and relieve a restless mind.

RECIPES TO VITALIZE AND MOTIVATE

To shift from a state of dullness and lethargy to a state of calm contentment, you need to focus on *moving the energy* first. Slow, dull mental space needs motivation more than anything. The recipes in chapter 10 make use of sour and spicy tastes such as lemon, red chili, and vinegar to awaken the mind and get the juices flowing. If a bogged-down physical state is contributing to your heavy mind-space, foods that lighten and cleanse the body—such as beets, sprouts, berries, and greens—will help to promote clarity. Astringent, pungent, and bitter foods support a bright and active mind by increasing agni through recipes like Spicy Turmeric Lemonade (see page 295) and Lemon Parsley Quinoa (see page 267). Use the recipes in this chapter when you are feeling sluggish in appetite or mental state to enliven your mind and encourage productivity. Once the flame of the mind is enkindled by these slightly fiery dishes, you can work toward a calm clarity without feeling sleepy or sad.

    This collection of recipes offers something for everyone, and most are easy to prepare. There's no need to be strict about it or perfect. Just try some sattvic cooking and see how much better you feel! Have fun, be a mad scientist in the kitchen, and get cooking.

In a Nutshell: Cooking for the Mind

———— ◆❖◆ ————

Each chapter of recipes begins by reviewing basic diet and lifestyle guidelines for balancing the maha gunas. While eating well is a key to balance, experimenting with the lifestyle guidelines will enhance your efforts exponentially. Integrating the recipes and daily recommendations from chapter 8 can bring balance in and of itself by cultivating a calm, clear state of awareness. But in the event that you are experiencing restless, anxious, or fiery energy in the mind or body, look to chapter 9. If it's lethargy and a heavy, dull energy that predominates, refer to chapter 10. If you are not quite sure what is going on, each chapter begins with a balance and imbalance table to help you recognize some telltale signs and symptoms of the energies that move the mind.

7

basic recipes
for the
sattvic kitchen

basic recipes

———— ◆ ◆ ◆ ————

These recipes are the foundation for creating sattvic soups, baking ingredients, spices, and sauces. In my own kitchen, I try to use the same nutritious staples—a small variety of grains, nuts, legumes, and seeds—in creative ways. This chapter covers how to sprout, culture, soak, and make fresh milks and flours. I count on these nourishing essentials, and then I vary the fruits and vegetables each time I go to the store, which keeps my shopping simple and my food fresh.

Many of these basics are things you might be used to buying packaged, like applesauce, spice blends, and almond milk. Wait until you make them at home—it is a game changer. Using freshly made staples ensures that all your food will be not only full-flavor, but also full-prana. You will find all of these basics easy to make and totally worth the effort. Once you catch a rhythm for busting out a nut milk every few days and grinding a monthly batch of fresh spice mix, you won't want the store-bought variety anymore.

MILKS

My partner, Rich, likes to poke fun at my milk obsession—I am always concerned with how much milk is left because I don't ever want to get caught without fresh milk for my morning tea (it's early!). I generally have two fresh nut milks going at one time, as one may be used for tea or bedtime tonic and the other for soups. I have included my favorite uses for each, and as you will discover, they work beautifully in many Ayurvedic dishes.

Note: All milks will store in the refrigerator for up to 7 days. Shake well before each use.

almond milk

MAKES 1 QUART

Slightly cooling and balancing for everyone, the soaked almond is revered in Ayurveda for nourishing the brain with good fats, keeping you steady and calm. Make this your go-to milk for a warm evening cup or a creamy base for soups. It is even refreshing served cool and gently sweetened with maple syrup and cardamom in hot weather.

²/₃ cup raw almonds, soaked overnight, drained, and rinsed

4 cups water

Dash of salt (optional)

Using a hand blender or a carafe blender, process the soaked almonds with 1 cup of the water until smooth. Add the remaining 3 cups of water and salt. Blend again until smooth and foamy. Strain the milk through a fine sieve, a double layer of cheesecloth, or a clean dishtowel (strain twice if you like it very smooth).

You can use the leftover almond pulp to add fiber to soups, chutneys, and smoothies. Spread the pulp on a baking sheet, and dry it out by baking at 200 degrees for 1 hour. The pulp can be frozen for later use. When using it in recipes that call for almond meal, sub in just ¼ cup for ¼ cup of the almond meal, as the fibrous nature of the pulp can affect the final product if it is not used sparingly.

rice milk

The lightest and easiest to digest of all the milks, rice milk refreshes and revitalizes by the glass or adds a creamy note when cooked into a breakfast cereal.

1 cup uncooked brown or white rice, soaked overnight, drained, and rinsed

4 cups water

Add the soaked rice and water to a blender. Process until smooth. Strain the milk through a fine mesh sieve, a double layer of cheesecloth, or a clean dishtowel. Store in the refrigerator for up to 7 days.

The remaining rice pulp may be cooked in a little water, with raisins and Sweet Spice Mix (see page 127) for a clean and warming breakfast.

Grab the Cow

——— ◆ ◆ ◆ ———

In my favorite Christmas movie of all time, Bing Crosby asks Rosemary Clooney to "grab the cow." Which means, "Bring the milk over here, please." They pour thick, creamy, 8-ounce glasses from a pitcher, and I am reminded of how many kids were required to get nutrition from that glass of milk every day. A generation ago, a lot of propaganda in this country from the wheat, meat, and dairy industries played into the construction of a problematic food pyramid. The question these days is: do we or do we not grab the cow?

Cow's milk is still a large part of the diet in many cultures, yet we seem to have a hard time digesting it. Ayurveda takes into account not only the natural qualities of a substance, but also how it is processed, to determine the overall effects it will have on your health. Homogenized dairy is much harder for most of us to digest than the fresh milk that leaves the fat molecules intact. Denatured fats are definitely a bad idea from an Ayurvedic standpoint, as they translate easily to ama, or toxicity.

To me, grass-fed cow's milk tastes the most like the milk I enjoy in India. When I'm making chai or hot cocoa in the cold weather, this is what I buy. If raw milk is available in your area, even better. Cow's milk is a homeopathic substance in the Ayurvedic diet, not necessarily a mainstay, so a daily 8-ounce glass is not required! The right amount of milk depends on your personal constitution and digestive strength and the qualities of the current season (dry and cold = more milk fats).

hemp milk

The minerals and fatty acids in hemp seeds repair brain tissue and improve memory. They make the most nutritious and nutty-tasting of all the milks. Hemp milk adds deep body to drinks and soups and is my personal favorite. The beneficial oils in the hemp seed perish at high temperatures, so do not boil this milk; instead, use it for smoothies or warm it gently for bedtime tonics and creamy soups.

| ½ cup shelled hemp seeds | 1 Tbsp maple syrup | 4 cups water |

Add hemp seeds and 1 cup of the water to a blender; process on high until a smooth paste forms. Add the rest of the water and the maple syrup; blend again to combine. Strain through a fine mesh sieve, a double layer of cheesecloth, or a clean dishtowel.

Discard the pulp or refrigerate it to add to hot cereal within 3 days.

GRAINS

Whole grains are the cornerstone of an Ayurvedic diet. Almost all main meals will feature a serving of grains accompanied by smaller flavorful side dishes and condiments. Here are a few options for grains with varying Ayurvedic qualities, so you can choose what suits you best and combine it with any of the legume and vegetable dishes. For digestibility, be sure to cook your grains fully, so they are soft and moist, not dry and sticky. You will enjoy an optimal digestive fire if you have unrefined, complex carbohydrates at warm, sit-down meals. Slower, heavier digestive systems will need less grain and should then include more cooked vegetables and legumes.

basmati rice

MAKES 3 CUPS

Hulled (white) basmati rice, the queen of grains, is prized for its digestibility thanks to light, cooling qualities. Unlike the sticky, dense qualities of short-grain or processed rice, basmati's delicate grains burn clean, which promotes sharp mental faculties. Choose this soft, smooth, comforting grain when your digestion is weak to ensure that your body can reap optimal nutrition without working too hard. Basmati rice is a good go-to when you are feeling stressed and in need of something sweet and simple. I like to add ¼ tsp ghee when cooking this dish to keep the pot from boiling over and to balance the dry quality of the grain.

Note: When your digestion is strong, go for brown basmati rice, but cook it for a full 45 minutes.

1 cup white basmati rice	¼ tsp ghee
2 cups water	¼ tsp salt

Using a fine mesh sieve, rinse the rice under cool, running water. Submerge the sieve—rice and all—in a bowl of cool water, allowing the rice to soak for 30 minutes. Drain the rice and rinse one last time under cool, running water until the water runs clear.

Add the rice to a medium-size saucepan with the 2 cups of water, ghee, and salt. Bring to a boil over medium-high heat. Cover, reduce the heat to low, and simmer for 17 minutes. Do not disturb the rice while it cooks—no peeking under the lid or stirring! After 17 minutes, remove from the heat. Let stand, covered, for 5 minutes.

Remove the lid, fluff with a fork, and serve.

quinoa

MAKES 3 CUPS

Quinoa ("KEEN-wah"), a super seed, is an ancient food from the Andes. It has become quite popular among vegetarians for its complete protein profile of amino acids. It has the light qualities of a seed, rather than the dense, heavy qualities of hearty grains like wheat and oats, which makes it a great choice in warmer weather. It also cooks faster than most grains!

Note: Be sure to rinse your quinoa well two or three times in cool water, as naturally occurring chemicals called saponins in the hull of the seed may irritate the digestive tract.

1 cup quinoa

2 cups water

Using a fine mesh sieve, rinse the quinoa under cool, running water. Combine the rinsed quinoa and 2 cups of water in a medium-size saucepan. Bring the water and quinoa to a boil over high heat, then reduce the heat to low, cover, and simmer for 15–20 minutes. When all the liquid has been absorbed, remove from the heat. Let stand, covered, for 5 minutes.

Remove the lid, fluff with a fork, and serve.

barley

Barley, what I like to call "the sinus buster," is special for its ability to remove excess water from the body. This can be helpful in addressing weight loss, congestion, dullness, and general feelings of heaviness. Light, dry qualities will reduce lassitude in the body and mind. I reach for this grain when my head feels gunked up and have it daily at one or two meals, until things clear up. Soak it overnight before cooking for the softest, creamiest final product.

1 cup barley

3 cups water

Using a sieve or colander, rinse the barley under cool, running water. Combine the rinsed barley and 3 cups of water in a medium-size saucepan. Bring to a boil over high heat, then reduce the heat to low, cover, and simmer for 40–50 minutes. When the barley has tripled in volume, remove from the heat. Let stand, covered, for 10 minutes. Remove the lid, drain any excess water from the barley, and fluff with a fork. Cooked barley should be chewy and soft.

If presoaking your barley, reduce the cooking time by half.

FLOURS

The sattvic nature of your food increases with the love and care you put into cooking. Grinding your own grains into flour takes only a minute or two and ensures a fresh, nutrient-rich product. It is really easy, and I recommend you grind fresh each time you are making a recipe using one of these flours. Make sure your blender carafe is completely dry before you begin.

oat flour

MAKES 1 CUP

I use oat flour for most of my baking. Its flavor is naturally sweet, blends well, and produces rich cookies and bars.

1 cup rolled oats

Blend on high in a dry blender for about 5 seconds, until the oats have formed a fine flour.

buckwheat flour

MAKES 1 CUP

This flour has a stronger taste than oat or rice, and I use it in small amounts in baking, but it is my favorite for dosa. A buckwheat dosa has a rich, nutty taste that goes well with a spicy chutney.

1 cup raw buckwheat groats

Blend on high in a dry blender for about 5 seconds, until the groats have formed a fine flour.

Note: You can use roasted buckwheat, called *kashi*, but it has a strong, roasted flavor that may overpower other tastes. Raw groats are a safe and more sattvic bet.

rice flour

MAKES 1 CUP

For grinding rice, you need a high-speed blender. If you don't own one, you will have to buy rice flour, preferably in the bulk bins at a natural foods market.

I have used a white rice flour for all the recipes. You can make this flour using ½ cup brown rice and ½ cup white. Your recipes will come out a little coarser. Personally, I like my dosa and dumplings a little heartier, but it's not for everyone. I recommend you start out working with white rice flour.

1 cup white rice

Put the rice in the freezer for about 15 minutes. Put the cooled rice into a blender and process on low for a few seconds, then increase to high speed. When the rice begins to break up, stop the blender and stir the contents. Repeat this process once or twice more, until the rice has been ground to a fine flour.

almond meal

MAKES 1 CUP

If you haven't tried baking with almond meal, it's time to start. You can easily create protein-rich, high-fiber treats that give conventional cookies a run for their money.

1 cup raw almonds

In a blender or food processor, process the almonds on high for a few seconds, until a fine meal forms. Do not overblend, or you might end up with almond butter—the oils will separate, and clumps will begin to form in your flour.

SPROUTS

Sprouting increases the available nutrients from legumes and reduces gas by "pre-digesting" the beans. Ayurveda considers sprouts medicinal, as each little legume contains all of the potential energy it takes to grow from a seed to a plant. Sprouts bring that kind of potential energy to *you*, and they are great mental motivators! If you have a hard time digesting beans, this could be a great way to add vegetarian protein to your diet.

There are so many beans and seeds you can sprout. I've included the mung beans and lentils because, while I have tried sprouting everything, these are the two I find easy and quick enough to keep doing. I throw them into kichari and grain dishes of all sorts. While the soaked almonds won't actually sprout, they go through a similar process of predigestion and make a stellar snack.

Be sure to start with beans that aren't old and stale. Shop somewhere with a good turnover in the bulk foods department—a place that is generally busy and has a large bulk section is likely to fit the bill. Old beans will refuse to sprout because they have lost their mojo.

sprouted mung beans

MAKES 2 CUPS

½ cup green mung beans

1½ cups water

Soak the beans in the water overnight. In the morning, drain and rinse the beans in a strainer or colander. Spread them out in a thin layer on the bottom of the strainer, place a wide bowl underneath to catch drips, and put a towel over the top. Leave them out on the counter all day and night to sprout.

The next morning, rinse and drain the sprouts again. Cover with a towel and repeat the process. Within 48 hours or so (depending on how warm your kitchen is), the beans will begin to grow little white tails. It's best to eat the sprouts before the tails grow longer than ¼ inch. If you are not ready to eat them, you can refrigerate them in a glass storage container for a few days.

sprouted lentils

½ cup green lentils

1½ cups water

Follow the instructions for Sprouted Mung Beans (see page 125). You should have sprouted lentils within 2 days.

Alternate mason jar method: Purchase a sprouting top for a 1-quart, wide mouth mason jar. This little plastic mesh top screws onto the jar for easy rinsing and draining. You can also place cheesecloth over the top of the jar and screw the metal ring on to keep it in place. Keep the jar top-down on your dish rack to drain after rinsing. Your sprouts will grow right there next to the sink.

soaked almonds

MAKES ½ CUP

Soaking almonds releases enzymes and makes them much easier to digest. These nuts make a great travel snack or a welcome protein addition to salads and smoothies.

¼ cup raw almonds

1 cup cool water

Soak the almonds in the water for 8 hours or overnight. Discard the soaking water, rinse the almonds, and slip the skins off. Enjoy immediately as an energizing snack.

They will keep for 2–3 days in the fridge in an airtight container.

SPICE MIXES

Spices are the most potent medicine. Freshly ground, a pungent taste like black pepper can blast through fog to get you motivated, while a bit of bitterness, as in coriander seeds, can calm agitation. These spice mixes will balance your meals and moods by bringing the benefits of the six tastes. To grind your own, you will need a mortar and pestle, an electric spice grinder, or a coffee grinder dedicated to the task.

sweet spice mix

MAKES ¼ CUP

This mixture showcases the sweet tasting spices that are prized for their ability to promote sattva with smooth, harmonious flavors. This mixture also aids in the digestion of sweet foods by gently enkindling digestive fire. Use this mix in hot cereal, spiced milks, baked goods, and anywhere you want a warm touch.

2 Tbsp ground cinnamon	1 Tbsp ground cardamom
2 Tbsp ground ginger	1 tsp grated nutmeg (optional)

Mix the ground spices together in a glass shaker jar.

sattvic spice mix

Support balance in your mind by harmonizing your palate. This savory mixture contains all six tastes to promote well-rounded qualities, and it can help you achieve balance in body and mind. Hing is traditionally used for its oniony flavor, replacing the stimulating heat of onions with a tasty yet calming spice. This mix is especially nice in dals and soups.

1 Tbsp coriander seeds	½ tsp salt	¼ tsp hing powder
1 Tbsp cumin seeds	2 tsp ground ginger	
1 tsp fennel seeds	1 Tbsp ground turmeric	

Roast the coriander, cumin, and fennel seeds in the same frying pan over medium heat. Stir constantly for approximately 3–5 minutes, until you can smell them. Cool and then grind these spices together with the salt, ginger, turmeric, and hing powder to a uniform powder.

calming spice mix

Each of the spices featured in this mixture has the ability to cool down your digestive tract. Excessive heat stimulates the mind and can create discomfort in the body. This tasty mix helps to keep your digestion cool, which calms both your gut and your mind.

1 Tbsp coriander seeds	1 tsp cumin seeds	½ tsp ground cardamom
1 tsp fennel seeds	1 Tbsp ground turmeric	

Roast the coriander, fennel, and cumin seeds in the same frying pan over medium heat. Stir constantly for approximately 3–5 minutes, until you can smell them. Cool and then grind these spices together with the turmeric and cardamom to a uniform powder.

vitalizing spice mix

When it comes to motivating tamas, or the dense, heavy qualities of your mind, spice it up! The pungency of this spice mix can melt away resistance and sluggishness while lighting your digestive fire.

1 tsp fenugreek seeds

1 Tbsp coriander seeds

1 Tbsp cumin seeds

1 Tbsp mustard seeds

¼ tsp ground cloves (or 1 whole clove if you're grinding your own)

1 tsp ground cinnamon

1 tsp freshly ground black pepper

¼ tsp hing powder (optional)

Roast the fenugreek seeds in a small frying pan over medium heat for approximately 3–5 minutes. Cool and then grind them to a powder using a mortar and pestle or a spice grinder.

Roast the coriander, cumin, and mustard seeds in the same frying pan over medium heat. Stir constantly for approximately 3–5 minutes, until you can smell them. Cool and then grind these spices together with the fenugreek and remaining spices to a uniform powder.

Medicinal Potency

— ◆ ◆ ◆ —

After grinding, a spice's potency lasts for one month. This means store-bought ground spices are old. You can still use spice mixes, but they will slowly lose their efficacy. You can taste the difference. Keep a few small, airtight, glass spice containers for storing your spice mixes. Whole spices are good for one year before grinding. (You can find suppliers of high-quality spices in the "Resources" section.)

OTHER ESSENTIALS

These basics are used often in my kitchen, and you will find that making them at home adds a whole new dimension to your diet. A soup with homemade broth, or almond milk with your own vanilla, will taste and feel deeply nourishing.

vegetable broth

MAKES 3½ CUPS

Vegetable broth can be enjoyed as a beverage with a meal, between meals, and while fasting. It is also used as the base for soups and in cooking grains and beans to add flavor and nutrition. Try keeping a bag of vegetable scraps (like kale stems and sweet potato skins) in the freezer so you can boil them with herbs or fresh ginger to make your own fresh broth. You can start from scratch, but I love being able to use scraps for this purpose.

5 cups roughly chopped vegetables, such as carrots, potatoes, leeks, kale, parsnips, fennel, and/or washed organic vegetable skins

2 Tbsp ghee

Handful of fresh herbs, such as thyme, rosemary, oregano, sage, or parsley (stems included) or 2-inch piece fresh ginger, washed and thickly sliced

½ tsp salt

Pinch of freshly ground black pepper

7 cups water

In a large, heavy-bottomed pot, cook the vegetables in the ghee over medium heat for 10 minutes, stirring occasionally, until they begin to soften. Add the fresh herbs or ginger, salt, black pepper, and water; bring to a boil. Reduce the heat to low and simmer, partially covered, for 60 minutes.

Remove from the heat, and strain through a (metal) mesh sieve into a glass bowl or other heatproof container, pressing on the vegetables with the back of a spoon to extract as much flavor as possible.

Allow the broth to cool and then transfer to storage jars. Refrigerate for up to 1 week. If freezing, use within 1 month.

applesauce

Applesauce is such a simple and delicious food. With their cooling, calming, and detoxifying nature, apples are a staple for lasting balance. I like pink applesauce, so I leave the skins on for their healthy fibers.

Note: If you are going to bake with the sauce, as some of my recipes call for, be sure to peel the apples so the fiber doesn't make your baked goods rough.

4 apples, peeled, cored, and cut into 1-inch pieces

½ cup water

Bring the apples and water to a boil in a medium-size saucepan. Reduce the heat to medium and simmer, partially covered, for 20–25 minutes. Remove from the heat.

Depending on the type of apples you used, you may need to blend them into a sauce. Softer varieties of apples will be ready to go straight from the pot. Keeps up to 1 week in a sealed glass jar in the refrigerator.

fresh yogurt

Freshly cultured milk is a staple of the sattvic diet. Especially in the case of an ungrounded mind, its stable qualities are indispensable. It appears at every meal in some form or other, and you will find it in many of my recipes. Fresh yogurt is a rich source of protein and probiotics. The beneficial effects of homemade yogurt on the gut can be quite profound. If you don't digest milk well, you may find that you can add it back into your diet when it is cultured. Raw milk is the very best option. Non-homogenized, grass-fed milk is the next best. It is worth the effort of making your own yogurt—once you get the hang of it and find the right method for setting, you will have one of the most amazing health foods at your fingertips.

4 cups organic whole milk

¼ cup whole-milk yogurt,
    containing active cultures

In a heavy saucepan with a lid, heat the milk to just below boiling (about 200 degrees) over medium heat. As the milk heats, stir occasionally with a metal spoon so the bottom does not scorch. Use a cooking thermometer to measure the temperature of the milk; this will give you the best results. The milk is close to boiling when you see lots of steam and it makes a low simmering sound.

Remove the milk from the heat and let it cool to approximately 115 degrees. Again, use the thermometer to measure the temperature. When it's ready, the liquid will feel just warm to the touch. As the milk cools, continue to stir it every so often to prevent a film from forming on top. If a film does form, gently remove with the spoon and discard. Be patient with these first steps, as heating and cooling times will vary. Be attentive and enjoy the process.

Whisk ½ cup of the warm milk with the yogurt until smooth. Return to the pot of warm milk, and gently whisk together until evenly distributed. Place the lid on your pot, put it inside the oven, and close the door (the oven should be *off*). The closed oven will help to insulate the pot and keep it warm as the cultures do their work of making yogurt. In a cool climate, you may also wrap your pot in towels before placing it in the oven to help keep the pot warm and encourage a thicker yogurt. Placing the pot inside a room temperature cooler will also work well.

Let rest in the oven for 4 hours to overnight. The longer you let the cultures work, the thicker and more tart your yogurt will become. When the yogurt is set to your liking, remove from the oven, pour into a sterilized glass jar or stainless steel container, and refrigerate for up to 2 weeks.

To make your next batch of yogurt, retain ¼ cup of your homemade yogurt and use it to start the next batch. You may need to begin from scratch after a few batches, as the culture can begin to lose its potency.

Note: Do not use ultra-pasteurized milk, as this milk has been through an extra heating process before sale and will not culture correctly. Pasteurized milk is okay.

Store-bought yogurt often contains pectin to artificially create a smoother, thicker product and to extend shelf life. Your homemade yogurt may appear thin, curdled, or clumpy, and this is as it should be! The taste will be far superior to and so much fresher than anything you buy at the supermarket.

No Thermometer?

——— ◆ ◆ ◆ ———

If you aren't sure you want to commit to buying a thermometer, you might try this. I first learned to make yogurt using the hot-finger thermometer. The milk has cooled to the correct temperature when you stick your finger in up to the second knuckle, and you think it's going to burn you, but it doesn't. This is the perfect temperature at which to add your culture. Stick your finger in slowly, so you don't get hurt.

ghee

Otherwise known as clarified butter, ghee is considered to be the most beneficial cooking medium in Ayurveda. This oil has the highest heat tolerance, is light enough to digest easily, and penetrates the body's tissues—providing the necessary nourishment where you need it most. Think of ghee as a carrier that brings goods deep into the body, including the brain. Quality fats bring the kind of moisture that keeps the mental muscles limber. Because ghee is seen as medicinal, only the best quality organic butter should be used to produce ghee.

What you are about to do here is remove the solids from the butter, leaving you with a golden yellow, spoonable cooking oil. As it cooks, the water will be released in the form of tiny bubbles, and the solids will separate and float on top (later they may sink). The trick is to catch it before it burns, so you must stay with the butter for the full 15 minutes it takes to separate. Watch it so you can see when the solids begin to brown. Once you get the hang of it, you can double the recipe and make it monthly.

Ghee is great used in place of butter for almost everything—toast, eggs, baked goods, or stirred into grains. It does have a strong flavor and a different texture, so it does not always work with traditional baking, but you will certainly find it in my recipes for baked goods!

½ lb unsalted organic butter
(2 sticks)

Place the butter in a saucepan over medium-low heat. When all the butter has melted, reduce the heat to low. After about 5 minutes, the butter will begin to form a white froth on its surface, and you will hear rapid popping sounds as the moisture evaporates. Continue to monitor the ghee; do not walk away or multi-task. Simmer for 10–15 minutes, listening attentively. Notice when the popping sounds become more intermittent, and then it's time to hover.

Check your ghee for doneness. Using a clean metal spoon, gently move the froth or bubbles to the side and take a look at the bottom of the pan. You should be able to see clearly through the yellow liquid; it will no longer be cloudy. When the solids on the bottom of the pan begin to turn golden brown and the ghee smells similar to toffee, remove from the heat.

Cool until it's just warm, about 15 minutes. Strain through a fine mesh metal strainer or a double layer of cheesecloth into a sterilized glass jar. Skim off any last bits of foam that might remain. Ghee does not need refrigeration for 1 month or so. (If it's around longer, store it in the fridge, but try to take it out when you start cooking, so it softens.) Keep it on the counter with the lid on. Always use a clean utensil when taking ghee from the jar.

pure vanilla essence

MAKES ABOUT 1 CUP

PREPARATION TIME: 1 MONTH

Making your own vanilla extract is very easy and a great way to ensure a pure product. Be sure to use a top-shelf alcohol and fair-trade vanilla beans. The tastiest vanilla comes from Madagascar, the world's leading producer. Skimping on quality for vanilla is not worth it in the end, and you'll find that making your own is ultimately less expensive. The extract is good for 1 year if you store it in an amber bottle and keep it out of the sun. Homemade vanilla in a decorative glass container with a ribbon makes an excellent gift for bakers.

5 vanilla beans

1 cup high-quality bourbon or vodka

Split the vanilla beans lengthwise and cut into 1- to 3-inch pieces (short enough to be completely submerged in your chosen vessel). Add the beans to a clean jar and pour in the bourbon or vodka. Seal the jar and store in a cool, dark place for 1 month. Visit the jar occasionally and give it a good shake. For a deeper flavor, allow it to sit for a longer period of time.

When the essence has achieved the desired flavor, pour it into an amber bottle and store in a cool, dark place. If you choose to strain the seeds out of your essence, use a coffee filter and funnel when transferring to the new bottle.

Note: Homemade extract is not as strong as store-bought concentrates, so you may find you need to use a little extra when baking.

home-roasted tahini (sesame paste)

MAKES 1 CUP

Sesame seeds are wonderful for building strength and vitality, especially in the reproductive tissues. This paste is a great one for making rich sauces and dressings and as a binder for baking nourishing, egg-free sweets. Home-roasted nuts and seeds are guaranteed to be much fresher and more sattvic than the store-bought variety.

1 cup white sesame seeds

¼–½ cup sesame oil (not toasted)

Warm a large, heavy-bottomed frying pan over medium heat. Cast-iron works great. Add the sesame seeds and stir continuously until they begin to brown and glisten, up to 10 minutes. Remove from the heat and allow to cool completely. This will happen faster if you transfer the seeds to a cool pan.

Pour the cooled seeds into a food processor or high-speed blender, and drizzle the sesame oil on top. Process until smooth, scraping the sides of the bowl frequently. If your paste seems too thick, continue to add sesame oil, a tablespoon at a time, up to ¼ cup. Sesame paste should be spreadable but a bit runny.

Transfer the paste to an airtight glass container. Refrigerate for up to 1 month.

Note: Unhulled, or brown, sesame seeds will produce a bitter final product. For increased fiber and nutrition, you can use half brown and half white. This recipe calls for only hulled, white sesame seeds and produces a fine, sweet paste.

basic coconut chocolate

This easy chocolate recipe is the base I use in all my chocolate treats, like Chocolate Mint Double-Dipped Strawberries (page 285) and Chocolate Layered Ojas Bars (page 195). Coconut butter holds its solidity at higher temperatures, but it's not as easy to digest as pure coconut oil, which is a great fat. I manage heat sensitivity by keeping chocolate confections in the refrigerator and usually make them in cool weather, when the heating quality of cacao is more appropriate.

½ cup melted coconut oil

½ cup cacao powder

3 Tbsp maple syrup

Melt the coconut oil by standing the jar in hot water. In a small bowl, whisk together the coconut oil, cacao, and maple syrup until smooth.

Pour this mixture into candy molds to make chocolates, spread on a baking sheet lined with wax paper for chocolate bark, or refrigerate in a jar and melt again for later use. Coconut chocolate can keep in the refrigerator for up to 6 weeks.

BASICS

Serving suggestion pictured (left): Chocolate Layered Ojas Bars

BASIC RECIPES FOR THE SATTVIC KITCHEN

8

---

recipes *for* sattva, contentment, *and* clarity

sattva

— ◆◆◆ —

Peace of mind is not complicated. It's simple. It's about easy breathing; smelling the roses; and moving at a steady, comfortable pace. Anchor this intention with a clean and nurturing diet and a little attention to self-care. Life gets crazy, I know. So these sattvic recipes are deeply nourishing and truly simple to prepare. Enjoy warm vegetable salads, protein-rich soups and stews, flourless treats, balancing beverages, and tangy condiments—all in the name of satisfaction! Use these recipes to harness the potential energy of your sattvic mind and bring a creative, sustainable spirit to your days.

cultivating sattva

——— ◆ ◆ ◆ ———

Sattva feels like:
Content, restful, peaceful, steady, satisfied, fulfilled

Signs of Mental Balance or Strong Sattva

- Ability to concentrate, as well as to shift the attention
- Ability to manifest and implement new ideas
- Self-confidence
- Satisfaction
- Participation with the exterior world, as well as the inner one
- Sound sleep
- Healthy, comfortable digestion (regular bowel movements, no hyperacidity)
- Sustained energy
- Compassion toward self and others
- Balance of work and play
- Stable emotions

Tastes to Enjoy

Sweet, smaller amounts of sour, salty, pungent, bitter, astringent

Foods to Favor

Vegetarian

Fresh, ripe, seasonal fruits

Fresh, local, seasonal vegetables (squashes, sweet potatoes, root vegetables)

Raw and home-roasted nuts and seeds

Well-cooked whole grains

Small beans (especially mung)

Small-batch oils

Ghee

Homemade food

Foods to Reduce

Leftovers (overnight)

Frozen, packaged, and processed foods

Wilted or old food

Restaurant food

Dry foods (chips, crackers, popcorn, cold cereal)

Eggs

Onions and garlic

White sugar

Overly salty, sour, spicy, or sugary foods

Drugs and alcohol

General Lifestyle Guidelines

Eat mostly home-cooked meals.

Enjoy creative, outdoor, and playful activities.

Follow a schedule that is early to bed, early to rise.

Keep your home and work spaces clean and tidy.

Practice yoga and meditation.

Take quiet, contemplative time every day.

Give gifts and serve others.

sattvic smoothie

Sustained energy from good fats, a dose of bitter, and a hint of sweet make this six-taste smoothie a sattvic star. The low-sugar content in berries makes them a good type of fruit to combine with other foods. I prefer to use water or coconut water rather than milk and to sweeten with honey. Ginger will warm this smoothie up, making it easier on the gut. No ice is nice!

1 cup blueberries	2 kale leaves	½ tsp ground ginger
2 Tbsp hemp seeds	1½ cups coconut water or	1 tsp raw honey (optional)
¼ avocado	plain water	

Place the ingredients in a blender in the order listed. Begin to pulse on low so the honey, if using, does not fly upward. Blend on high for 1 minute.

Pour into 2 glasses and serve immediately.

The Avocado Question

———— ◆ ◆ ◆ ————

Avocados are earthy, heavy, and oily, which can lend them both rajasic and tamasic qualities. At the same time, their naturally occurring vegetable fat nourishes the body and can replace dairy for those who do not digest it well. In this recipe, I've paired a small amount of avocado, just enough to add some grounding and creamy texture, with the light qualities of berries and kale. I don't recommend relying on this for breakfast every day, but I do want to demonstrate a dairy-free smoothie option that won't freeze your gut.

ginger carrot muffins

MAKES 6 MUFFINS

I like my baked goods to be a meal unto themselves. I call these "food-muffins." Unlike the empty calories of flour and sugar pastries that send you straight into a midmorning crash, these muffins have a hearty dose of protein, fiber, good fat, and even vegetables! A breakfast that creates sustained energy is nonnegotiable for those who need to engage their minds in the morning. Feel good about having a muffin and milky tea for breakfast—eat two and make it all the way to lunch without a snack.

1 Tbsp ground chia seeds	½ tsp baking soda	**mix-ins**
3 Tbsp water	1 tsp baking powder	1 Tbsp minced fresh ginger
¾ cup almond meal	¼ cup maple syrup	¾ cup shredded carrot
¾ cup rolled oats	½ cup applesauce	¼ cup raisins
¼ tsp salt	2 Tbsp coconut oil, melted	
¼ tsp ground turmeric		

Preheat oven to 350 degrees. Line muffin tins with baking cups.

In a medium-size bowl, whisk together the chia seeds and water. Let stand for 5 minutes. In a separate bowl, mix the almond meal, rolled oats, salt, turmeric, baking soda, and baking powder.

Add the maple syrup, applesauce, and coconut oil to the chia seeds and whisk with a fork until well combined. Mix in the ginger and shredded carrot. Add the dry ingredients to the wet and mix together, then fold in the raisins.

Divide the batter among 6 muffin cups, and bake for 25–30 minutes, or until golden brown. These muffins are best served warm.

Dinacharya: Integrating Daily Self-Care

———— ✦ ◆ ✦ ————

While on the topic of breakfast, let's discuss what happens *before* the first meal of the day. *Dinacharya* means "daily regimen." Routines such as *abhyanga* (oil massage), nasal irrigation, and tongue scraping assist the body in eliminating wastes that have accumulated during the night and prepare it for the day ahead. For your general health and longevity, the regimen includes morning routines that care for the five sense organs: the skin, eyes, ears, nose, and mouth. (Instructions on how to perform these practices can be found in appendix 1.)

date pear morning kichari

There is something fabulous about the sweet combination of dates and pears. The pear is light, cool, and balancing to all body types, while dates add density to get you through to lunch. The glory of this recipe is learning how to prepare a delicious kichari for breakfast and enjoying all the health benefits of this nourishing superfood at any time of day.

Note: Dates can be replaced with raisins for those in need of a lighter-quality dish.

½ cup basmati rice	4 cups water	4 Medjool dates, pitted
½ cup yellow split mung	2 tsp Sweet Spice Mix	and chopped
beans, soaked overnight	2 pears, cored and chopped	½ tsp salt
or at least a few hours	into ½-inch cubes	1 Tbsp coconut oil

Rinse the rice and mung beans well. In a medium saucepan, bring the water, rice, and mung beans to a boil on high heat. Reduce heat and let simmer, uncovered, for 15–20 minutes.

Add the spice mix, pears, and dates. Cover and simmer 15–20 minutes more, adding more water if needed. Go for the consistency of thick oatmeal. When the kichari reaches the right consistency, turn off the heat and stir in the salt and coconut oil.

Let stand for 5 minutes before eating.

Kichari: It's Not Just for Cleansing Anymore

— ◆ —

This one-pot, complete-protein meal is so simple to make. I am struck by how often people tell me, "OK, I've got the soups and the kichari down, but I'm stuck on what to eat for a hot breakfast." When you're kicking the cold-cereal habit, and oatmeal is feeling a little heavy or more protein is in order, try this recipe or Apple Raisin Breakfast Kichari (page 216) to get you started on creative, balancing breakfasts.

rice flour breakfast crepe (dosa) with savory coconut chutney

SERVES 2–3

Dosa ("DO-sah") is an amazing food! This Indian crepe can be enjoyed at any meal. As a savory, vegan breakfast, it stands in well for bready, sugary pancakes. I like to serve this dosa with dal for a complete protein. Any of the chutney and pickle recipes also complement dosa if you want lighter fare. The batter will keep for 5 days in the fridge and may require a little more water to thin it out after it sits. If you mess up the first one, don't worry, we all do.

RICE FLOUR BREAKFAST CREPE

1 cup rice flour

½ cup whole-milk yogurt, whisked with a fork

¼ tsp cumin seeds

¼ tsp salt

1 Tbsp finely chopped cilantro leaves (optional)

¾ cup water

Coconut oil or ghee for frying

Mix together the rice flour, yogurt, cumin seeds, salt, and cilantro (if using) until smooth. Add the water, ¼ cup at a time, until the consistency is slightly thinner than pancake batter. The amount of water will vary with different rice flours. Let stand for 10 minutes.

Heat a large, ceramic, nonstick frying pan on medium-high heat. The pan is ready when you flick water on it and it sizzles immediately. Add ½ tsp oil to the pan.

Ladle about ¼ cup of the batter into the pan and quickly spread it into a circle using the back of a large spoon. Fill in any spaces with extra batter. Cover loosely with a lid to steam as you fry. Cook until the edges are brown and a spatula will slide under the dosa, about 3–4 minutes. Flip, and brown the other side for about 1 minute.

Serve immediately.

SAVORY COCONUT CHUTNEY

SERVES 4–6

Coconut chutney is ubiquitous in southern India and shows up at breakfast, dinner, and snacktime. The beneficial oils of the coconut mixed with warming spices make a simple, digestible chutney that goes best with dosas. Make just enough, as this one doesn't keep well for long.

1½ cups desiccated coconut	½-inch piece fresh ginger, peeled	**tempering (optional)**
1½ cups warm water		1 Tbsp coconut oil
1 green chili, sliced in half and seeded (optional)	¼ tsp ground coriander	1 tsp black mustard seeds
	½ tsp salt	¼ tsp hing powder

In a food processor or blender, grind all the chutney ingredients together to make a smooth paste. You will have to stop the blender and scrape down the sides a few times.

Serve in a small cup alongside the dosa.

Note: If you are using a subpar blender and the texture comes out course, try soaking the coconut in the water for 20 minutes first.

To get fancy:

Transfer the chutney into individual serving bowls.

In a small frying pan, heat the oil on medium heat. Add the mustard seeds and hing, and stir gently until they splutter. Cover the pan and fry for 1 minute. Remove from the heat and pour the tempering over each chutney bowl.

Serve immediately on the plate beside the dosa.

A fresh young coconut is green on the outside. Inside, however, is a fibrous brown shell. The shell dries up when aged, and the meat becomes sweet, good for grating and cooking. You have probably seen hard, brown coconuts at the grocery store. Most of us don't have the tools to crack the shell or grate the meat. If you live in a climate where coconuts grow, I do hope you take time to learn about their uses and preparation. For the rest of us, fresh coconut meat can be found in the frozen foods section at Indian grocers and health food stores. In a pinch, dried, unsweetened coconut will also work here. Soak the dried coconut in a few tablespoons of warm water while you prepare everything else, and it will meld into the chutney nicely.

KICHARI FOUR WAYS

Maintaining a pure vegetarian, sattvic diet requires regular sit-down meals that provide complete nutrition. You will notice it is a light diet compared to most modern fare, and you need to take care to nourish your body well to avoid falling on the chocolate bars and burgers or ending up depleted, which leads to its own imbalances in the body and mind. These four recipes for one-pot, complete-protein cooking with varying grains, legumes, and flavor profiles are easy to prepare and absolutely satisfying. Check out all the kichari recipes one by one, and you will be cooking up kichari several times a week for breakfast, lunch, or dinner and feeling energized, comfortable, and in balance.

Why Is Kichari so Important?

— ◆ ◆ ◆ —

Kichari ("Kich-AH-ree"), also spelled *kichadi*, is a porridge made of beans and rice. The traditional, cleansing version is made with split mung beans and white basmati rice, as in Calming Kichari (page 219). This combination, when cooked well with plenty of water, ghee, and digestive spices, both nourishes and cleanses the body without supporting any kind of imbalance. This easy-to-digest dish is beneficial for all body types and all seasons. Kichari works well when the digestion is "off" in any way or the mind and emotions are unsteady.

Kichari Love

— ◆ ◆ ◆ —

If you've undertaken a "kichari-cleanse," the modern take on cleansing from an Ayurvedic perspective, keep this in mind: While it is more grounding and nourishing than juicing or fasting, it can create a bit of an, um, kichari aversion. I experienced it myself in the beginning and have heard this from many clients. Hang in there—it may take a year or so, but in a state of balance, your body will begin to crave the superfood combo.

butternut kichari

SERVES 4–6

This is a fall favorite of mine. The roasted squash stirs into the body of the kichari for a sweet, creamy, orange festival in a bowl. Make sure you cook this stew to an absolute puree for the best results.

1 small butternut squash	¾ cup basmati rice	¼ cup coconut, large flakes,
Coconut oil	1 Tbsp Sweet Spice Mix	for garnish
4 cups water	1 tsp ground turmeric	
1 can full-fat coconut milk	2-inch piece fresh ginger,	
¾ cup split mung beans,	peeled and finely diced	
soaked overnight or at	1 tsp salt	
least a few hours		

To roast the squash: Preheat oven to 400 degrees. Cut the squash in half, scoop out the seeds, rub a few drops of coconut oil onto the cut faces, and place face-up on a baking sheet. Roast until tender, about 1 hour. Remove from the oven.

In a large saucepan, bring 3 cups of the water and the coconut milk to a boil on high heat. Set the other cup of water aside to add during cooking as needed.

Rinse the mung beans and rice well. Add the rice, beans, spice mix, turmeric, and ginger to the boiling water. Keep on high heat until the liquid boils again. Turn the heat down to low.

Scoop the squash out of the skin with a large spoon and add, in chunks, to the pot. The chunks will break down as it cooks. Simmer, partially covered, for 40 minutes or more, adding the reserved 1 cup water as needed. It's finished when the rice and mung beans are soft; the liquid is loose and soupy; and the butternut squash chunks have fallen apart. Turn off the heat, and stir in the salt. Let stand, covered, for 5 minutes.

In a frying pan, toast the coconut flakes on medium heat, stirring until they begin to brown. Remove from the heat immediately. Spoon the kichari into individual bowls and garnish each bowl with 1 Tbsp coconut flakes.

sprouted mung bean kichari

SERVES 6

In its simplicity, this dish is a model of the sattvic diet: fresh sprouts, moderately spiced and simply prepared. This is one of my go-to recipes, as quick as it is nutritious—all the goodness of mung beans without an extended cooking time. You may add a vegetable to steam on top during simmering, if you like. Serve with Lemon Pickle, a chutney, or a relish.

6 cups water

¾ cup green mung beans, sprouted (see page 125)

¾ cup basmati rice

1 Tbsp Sattvic Spice Mix

2-inch piece fresh ginger, peeled and finely diced

1 tsp salt

1–2 Tbsp ghee

Fresh cilantro, for garnish

In a large saucepan, boil 5 cups of the water on high heat. Set the other cup aside to add during cooking as needed.

Cover the mung beans with water and agitate with your fingers. Skim off any skins that float to the top, and drain off the water. Rinse the rice twice or until the water runs clear.

Add the rice, beans, spice mix, and ginger to the boiling water. Keep on high heat until the liquid boils again. Turn the heat down to low and simmer, partially covered, until moist and creamy, 20–30 minutes. Add a little more hot water if the kichari appears dry. Turn off the heat, and stir in the salt and ghee. Let stand, covered, for 5 minutes.

Serve with fresh cilantro and a side of seasonal steamed vegetables. I often choose kale, carrots, or sweet potatoes.

Why Mung Beans?

— ◆ ◆ ◆ —

Ayurveda adores the mung bean, which does not promote any imbalance in any body type. These small, green, round guys are a building food, yet they are light to digest. For these reasons, mung is used during detoxification periods to nourish the body, while allowing the digestive tract to do its cleanup. To see what mung beans look like whole and split, refer to this photo.

wild rice kichari

I love putting wild rice in kichari for its chewy texture. In this recipe, I'm offering a Thanksgiving remembrance with cranberries and squash. Just the right amount of wild rice is the key. Wild rice is excellent because it presents as an aromatic, chewy grain with lots of flavor, but it's a berry! As such, it has light, sattvic qualities. Soaking is a must to soften its black husk and render the grains easily digestible. Soak the mung beans and rice together to shorten prep time.

6 cups water	⅔ cup white basmati rice	¼ cup fresh (or frozen)
½ cup split yellow mung	1 Tbsp Sweet Spice Mix	cranberries, finely
beans, soaked overnight	1 cup cubed butternut	chopped
in 1 cup water	squash	1 tsp salt
⅓ cup wild rice, soaked	1 Tbsp maple syrup	1–2 Tbsp ghee
overnight in 1 cup water		

In a large saucepan, boil 5 cups of the water on high heat. Set the other cup aside to add during cooking as needed.

Rinse and drain the beans and wild rice. Wash the basmati rice well.

Add the rices, beans, spice mix, and squash to the water. Keep on high heat until it boils again. Immediately turn the heat down and simmer, partially covered, for 30 minutes. Do not stir.

After 20 minutes, add the maple syrup and cranberries. If the beans are not submerged, add another cup of water, but do not stir. Simmer, covered, for 10 more minutes. Take off the heat. Stir in the salt and ghee as you mix the cooked squash and cranberries to a uniform texture.

Serve in bowls with a tablespoon of Cranberry Orange Raisin Relish or cranberry sauce, if you like.

hearty french lentil kichari

This is a hearty, fiber-rich kichari seasoned with the cozy, satisfying tastes of tamari and *ajwain* (bishop's weed). The result of combining the nourishing French lentil and brown rice with rich seasonings and kale makes a great cold-weather lunch to ground and sustain you for the rest of the afternoon.

---

6 cups water

1 cup brown basmati rice, rinsed and soaked overnight

1 cup French (Le Puy) lentils, rinsed and soaked overnight

1 Tbsp Sattvic Spice Mix

2 cups chopped kale, large stems removed

1 Tbsp tamari

Fresh cilantro, for garnish

tempering

1–2 Tbsp ghee

½ tsp ajwain (optional; if you can't find it, replace with cumin seeds)

1 tsp mustard seeds

In a large saucepan, boil 5 cups of the water on high heat. Set the other cup aside to add during cooking as needed.

Rinse and drain the rice and lentils. Add the spice mix, rice, and lentils to the water. Keep on high heat until it boils again. Immediately turn the heat down and simmer, partially covered, for 30 minutes. Do not stir. Check after the first 20 minutes to see if the beans are submerged. If not, pour the other cup of water on top, and do not stir. Put the kale on top to steam. Cover and simmer for 10–20 minutes more. The texture should look loose, and the rice and lentils should be breaking down.

Warm the ghee in a small skillet on medium heat. Add the ajwain (if using) and mustard seeds. When the seeds pop, about 2–3 minutes, take off the heat, and pour into the kichari. Add the tamari and stir well. Let stand, covered, for a few minutes.

Served as a stew, kichari should have a soupy, soft consistency. Garnish with fresh cilantro if you have it.

gingered sweet potato dal

SERVES 4

You are going to like this one. After a crazy day, it makes such a comforting, stabilizing evening meal. Excellent for building muscle and satisfying big appetites, the lentils and sweet potato combine for an incredibly nourishing soup. It is enough to make a meal, especially with a side of steamed greens.

1 Tbsp coconut oil

3-inch piece fresh ginger, peeled and coarsely chopped

½ tsp ground cinnamon

2 tsp Sattvic Spice Mix

1 cup red lentils

4 cups water

1 medium sweet potato, skinned and diced into ½-inch pieces (about 1½ cups)

¾ cup almond, oat, or cow's milk

½ tsp salt

Freshly ground black pepper to taste

Warm the coconut oil in a large saucepan. Sauté the ginger, cinnamon, and spice mix in the oil until you can smell the spices; stir gently so the spices don't stick to the bottom.

Add the lentils, and sauté for 1–2 minutes, stirring until coated. Add the water and diced sweet potato. Bring to a boil, then turn the heat to low, cover partially, and simmer for 20–30 minutes. Turn off the heat, and add the milk and salt.

Using a hand blender, puree the soup to a chunky texture. You can also do this by blending half the soup in the carafe of a blender and then adding it back to the rest. If using a blender, you must cool the mixture a bit before blending; the milk should cool it down.

Serve with dosa or rice.

How Much Should I Eat?

— ◆ ◆ ◆ —

- According to the ancient information, the amount of food you eat at a meal should fit into the bowl shape made by holding your two hands together side by side.
- The first belch occurs when the air shifts around to accommodate the space in your stomach filling up. This is a sign it's time to call it a meal.
- Noticing when you are full takes presence and practice. Let this habit grow gradually.

steamed rice dumplings (kolukattai) with beet chutney

SERVES 3–4 (ABOUT 8 DUMPLINGS)

Kerala's local cuisine is known for delectable rice and coconut treats. These coconut-inspired dumplings are easy and fun to make. Enjoy them paired with vegetable soup or pack in your lunch box with chutney.

STEAMED RICE DUMPLINGS

¼ cup desiccated coconut

1 cup rice flour

1 tsp salt

1 Tbsp Sattvic Spice Mix

¾ cup water

¼ cup chopped cilantro

2 Tbsp coconut oil

1 tsp mustard seeds

1 Tbsp split mung beans, soaked overnight or at least a few hours

Put the coconut in a large bowl and set aside. In a large mixing bowl, combine the rice flour, salt, and spice mix. Work ¾ cup of the water into the flour mixture until a thick dough begins to form. With a spatula or your hands, work the cilantro into the dough, adding more water if necessary, until the dough is the consistency of cookie batter.

In a large frying pan or wok, heat 1 Tbsp of the oil over medium heat. Cook the mustard seeds until they pop, then add the split mung dal and stir constantly just until the dal begins to brown. Pour into the large bowl with the coconut.

In the same frying pan, warm another 1 Tbsp of the oil over medium heat. Add the rice mixture and stir, heating for 4–5 minutes. It should look dry and crumbly. Remove from the heat and add to the bowl with the coconut, dal, and mustard seeds. Allow to cool for a few minutes.

Mix the cooled dough with a spatula or your hands until the dal and coconut are evenly spread throughout the dough. To test the dough, take a handful (about ½ cup) and squeeze it in your hand to see if it sticks together. If it's too dry and crumbly, add water, a tablespoon at a time, until the dough is manageable. Squeeze the dough gently in your palm to shape it into half-moon dumplings. They will have finger marks. Place the dumplings in a steaming basket with enough water to steam over high heat for 5 minutes.

Serve hot with Beet Chutney, Your Daily Dal, or Vegetable Cilantro Raita.

BEET CHUTNEY

MAKES ABOUT 1 CUP

The creamy pink color of this chutney does wonders for the eyes and rounds out a plate of grains and greens with color and a tantalizing bit of sweetness. It is pleasing and balancing, with its bright, sweet, and grounding qualities. I highly recommend using curry leaves, fresh or frozen, if you can get them.

1 Tbsp coconut oil	3–4 curry leaves or bay leaf
1 tsp cumin seeds	(crumble a piece the size
1 tsp split mung beans,	of a pinky nail)
soaked overnight or at	1 cup grated beets
least a few hours	¼ cup full-fat coconut milk

In a medium frying pan, warm the oil on medium heat. Sauté the cumin seeds, split mung beans, and curry leaves or bay leaf until you can smell them, 2–3 minutes. Add the beets and mix, stirring constantly until the beets are warm. Take off the heat and cool completely.

In a food processor, add the coconut milk to the beet mixture and grind briefly to make a paste. Serve at room temperature alongside dosa, dumplings, rice dishes, and steamed bitter greens.

You can refrigerate the chutney for up to 7 days.

spiced ghee rice with cumin roasted vegetables

SERVES 2–4

The spices in this rice create a luxurious aroma and a beautiful side dish. I make this one when I want my usual dal and rice to feel special.

SPICED GHEE RICE

Boiling peppercorns with the rice adds flavor without heat, and the addition of ghee to the rice reduces the dry quality, aiding digestion and absorption. You may want to remove the peppercorns before serving if you find them too spicy. They will rise to the top during cooking.

1 Tbsp ghee	2 cups water	4 peppercorns
2 tsp cumin seeds	2 cinnamon sticks	½ tsp salt
1 cup basmati rice, rinsed twice		

Warm the ghee in a 2-quart pot on medium heat. Add the cumin seeds and sauté until you can smell them, 1–2 minutes. Add the rice, and sauté until the grains are coated. Add the water, cinnamon sticks, and peppercorns, turn the heat to high, and bring to a boil. Reduce the heat and simmer, covered, for 20 minutes.

Take off the heat, add the salt, and fluff with a fork. Remove the cinnamon sticks before serving.

CUMIN ROASTED VEGETABLES

SERVES 2–4

While I've called for carrots here, you can roast any fall vegetables with this recipe: beets, sweet potatoes, parsnips. Roasting brings out the sweetness in vegetables and makes them quite a treat. It really reflects the importance of taking time to bring out the best in your food. Whether you are preparing food to share or simply your daily meals, I think you will find roasting an easy way to enhance seasonal vegetables.

1 lb carrots, peeled	½ tsp ground coriander	2 Tbsp fresh cilantro,
2 Tbsp ghee, melted	¼ tsp salt	roughly chopped
½ tsp cumin seeds		

Preheat the oven to 425 degrees. Slice the carrots in quarters lengthwise. Place in a large bowl, pour in the ghee, and toss to coat. Sprinkle with the cumin seeds, coriander, and salt; toss again to spread the spices evenly throughout. Use your hands if need be. Spread on a large roasting pan, and roast for 20 minutes, stirring halfway through.

Remove from the oven, and sprinkle with the chopped cilantro before serving.

mung bean fritter

I reach for this one when I need comfort food, especially when I need something restorative after a full day of teaching. This recipe is inspired by a baked, north Indian savory snack called handvo. Hailing from Gujarat, this spicy lentil/vegetable cake makes a hearty meal in itself, served with almond-cilantro or mint chutney. This stovetop preparation will remind you of making a frittata with mung beans instead of eggs.

1 cup split green mung beans, soaked over night	2 Tbsp chopped cilantro	**tempering**
	2 cups chopped spinach	1 Tbsp + 1 tsp ghee
1 Tbsp lemon juice	1 tsp Sattvic Spice Mix	½ tsp mustard seeds
2 Tbsp Fresh Yogurt	½ tsp salt	
¼ tsp baking soda		

Drain and rinse the mung beans. Using a food processor or high-speed blender, pulse to puree the beans, lemon juice, and yogurt. Transfer the mung bean mixture to a medium-size mixing bowl. Combine all the other ingredients with the ground mung beans. The mixture should be the consistency of thick pancake batter. If it's too thick, add water, a tablespoon at a time, until it's the correct consistency.

Warm the ghee in a medium, ceramic, nonstick frying pan or wok on medium heat. Sauté the mustard seeds in the ghee until they pop. Pour the mung bean mixture over the ghee, and spread evenly across the bottom of the pan with the back of a serving spoon.

Cover and cook over medium heat until the sides begin to brown, 3–6 minutes. Turn heat down a bit if the sides are browning too quickly and the center remains liquidy. Lift and flip the fritter by using two large spoons or spatulas, if necessary, to catch each side and avoid breaking. Cover and cook 10 minutes more, until golden brown. The final product should be an 8-inch disk, about 1 inch thick.

Take off the heat and transfer to a serving platter. Cut into bite-size squares or "pizza slices." Serve with Mint Chutney (see page 231).

sattvic noodle bowl

SERVES 4

This bowl of goodness is sure to hit the spot in cooler weather. Colorful, fresh, and free of excessive salt and vinegar, it will make you feel warmed but not overheated. The warm, moist qualities of sesame thicken the sauce and bring sustained energy to the mind. This brain food is a very good dish for an afternoon of studying or other focused work. Sometimes I add cubed tofu to the roasting pan for an added dose of protein.

1 bunch broccoli, cut into small florets (about 2½ cups)	Juice of ½ lime	1 Tbsp sesame seeds, toasted
1 cup red cabbage, roughly chopped	2 Tbsp sesame oil	¼ cup fresh cilantro, roughly chopped
1 Tbsp olive oil	¼ cup tahini	
¼ tsp salt	2 Tbsp tamari	
	1 tsp freshly grated ginger	
	One 8-oz package buckwheat soba noodles	

Preheat oven to 375 degrees. In a medium bowl, toss the broccoli and cabbage in the olive oil; sprinkle with salt. Spread on a rimmed baking sheet and roast for 12–15 minutes, stirring halfway through. Remove from the oven.

While the veggies are roasting, make the sauce. Combine the lime juice, sesame oil, tahini, tamari, and ginger in a small jar. Screw on the lid and give it a good shake, until all ingredients are mixed well.

Meanwhile, bring a pot of water to boiling and add the soba noodles. Cook until al dente, according to the package directions. Drain well.

Chop the roasted broccoli and cabbage into small pieces, and toss together with the noodles and sauce in a large bowl. Garnish with sesame seeds and cilantro.

baked polenta with kale pesto

SERVES 2–4

I love this simple casserole for its New England flavor. Corn is one of the original foods of the Americas, and anyone with an herb garden knows how much basil likes it here too. Local foods are as fresh as they come, and fresh food is key to staying in a positive energy zone. Look for non-GMO cornmeal and small-batch olive oil. Make your own garlic-free pesto and freeze some for next time, as too much garlic excites the mind. I recommend this dish for entertaining, as it looks fancy and colorful, but you certainly don't need to have company to enjoy something fancy.

polenta

4 cups water

1 cup coarsely ground
   cornmeal

1 tsp salt

2 Tbsp ghee

pesto

2 cups packed fresh kale
   leaves, about ½ bunch

½ cup packed fresh basil
   leaves

⅓ cup walnuts, toasted

¼ cup extra virgin olive oil

1 Tbsp lemon juice

1 tsp raw honey

¼ tsp sea salt

2 Tbsp nutritional yeast

Preheat oven to 350 degrees. In a 2-quart baking dish, stir together the water, cornmeal, and salt for the polenta. The cornmeal will sink to the bottom, which is normal. Place the baking dish on an upper rack in the oven and bake for 45 minutes. Remove from the oven and add the ghee, stirring until the ghee is melted. Return to the oven to bake for an additional 45–60 minutes.

While the polenta bakes, prepare the pesto. In a food processor, pulse the kale, basil, and walnuts until finely chopped. With the motor running, drizzle in the oil, lemon juice, and honey. Then add the salt and nutritional yeast, processing until all ingredients are combined.

The polenta is fully baked when it begins to get dry on top and jiggles only slightly when touched. Remove from the oven, and give one final stir. Allow to rest 10 minutes.

Serve in squares or wedges, topped with dollops of warm pesto.

toasted coconut and cumin pea soup

SERVES 2

This one is easy, delicious, and perfect for the spring and fall, when these green veggies are in season. Peas, in excess, can be rajasic, due to their tendency to cause wind. It is best to serve them fresh, warm, and gently cooked; even so I recommend using half peas and half green beans in this recipe to ensure a peaceful experience.

1 cup water	1 cup green beans, coarsely	2 Tbsp shredded coconut
1 cup full-fat coconut milk	chopped	Freshly ground black pepper
½ tsp salt	1 cup fresh peas	to taste
½ tsp cumin seeds		

In a medium saucepan, bring the water, coconut milk, salt, and cumin seeds to a boil on medium heat. Add the vegetables, allow to boil again, then turn the heat down. Simmer, covered, for 10 minutes. Remove from the heat and, using a hand blender or high-speed blender, puree the soup until smooth. Cover.

In a small frying pan, toast the coconut over medium-low heat, stirring constantly, until it begins to brown. This will take just a few minutes. Remove from the heat immediately.

Divide the soup into two bowls, and top each with 1 Tbsp of the toasted coconut and fresh ground pepper, to taste.

Note: Desiccated coconut in the tiny pieces won't give you any crunch. If you can find grated coconut or chips, where the pieces are a little bigger, they will give you a better texture for soup topping.

a sattvic caesar salad

In hot weather, crunchy, watery, leafy romaine lettuce feels like a perfect choice. But if you eat too many raw vegetables, without a balance of grounding qualities, the mind eventually becomes unsteady. Look no further for the perfect salad! I mix in some kale to get the deep green energy. I toss it with this creamy dressing and let it stand for a few minutes while I toast the pumpkin seeds. I sprinkle the seeds on while they're still hot so the greens soften a bit. For a substantial meal, I have this salad with Simple Stovetop Tofu (see *The Everyday Ayurveda Cookbook*) on top.

salad

One head romaine

2 cups baby kale

¼ cup toasted pumpkin
    seeds

Chop the tips off the romaine if any are brown. Remove the bottom 2 inches, and chop the remainder into bite-size pieces. Toss with the baby kale.

caesar dressing

½ cup raw pumpkin seeds

2 Tbsp tahini

¼ cup olive or flax oil

2 Tbsp nutritional yeast

¼ cup fresh lemon juice

1 Tbsp apple cider vinegar

1 tsp salt

½ tsp freshly ground black
    pepper

¼ cup water (plus an
    additional ¼ cup water
    on the side for processing
    if needed)

Place all of the dressing ingredients in the blender in the order listed. Pulse on low a few times, then increase the speed to high and blend for 1 minute. If the dressing looks too thick, add more water, a tablespoon at a time, until you have the desired consistency.

Pour the dressing over the salad and toss. Sprinkle with toasted pumpkin seeds, and plate immediately.

sattvic vegetable kofta

SERVES 4 (ABOUT 20 BALLS)

I have so many friends who go to Indian restaurants in search of kofta, which may be vegetarian but is too heavy and spicy to be truly sattvic. I have created kofta-lite. It's still a bit of work and still fried, but this is one of those special recipes you can make for a treat. Better yet, when you get the hang of making these balls, the sky is the limit for enjoying these falafel-like friends! This recipe cuts out some of the heating ingredients such as chili, garlic, and onions, but I have still included a lot of the traditional spices in the gravy.

kofta balls	curry	
2 cups water	1 tomato	3 green cardamom pods, cracked
1 cup dried mung beans, soaked overnight	1 leek	2 cloves
1 Tbsp Sattvic Spice Mix	4 celery stalks	1 tsp mustard seeds
½ tsp freshly ground black pepper	4-inch piece fresh ginger, peeled and finely chopped	3 peppercorns
½ tsp ground ginger	¼ cup water, plus an additional 3 cups	1 Tbsp Sattvic Spice Mix
½ tsp salt	1 Tbsp ghee	1 tsp ground turmeric
2 Tbsp ghee		1 tsp salt
		Fresh cilantro to garnish

For the kofta:

In a large saucepan, bring the 2 cups of water to a boil on high heat. Drain and rinse the mung beans, then add to the water. Reduce the heat, cover, and simmer 45 minutes. Remove from the heat, and drain off any excess water. Set aside to cool. Now is a good time to start the gravy.

For the gravy:

While the mung beans are cooling, coarsely chop the tomato, leek, and celery. Pulse the vegetables and ginger with the ¼ cup of water on high to a salsa-like consistency. Add a little more water if your blender is struggling.

Warm the ghee in a medium saucepan on medium heat. Sauté the cardamom, cloves, mustard seeds, and peppercorns in the ghee until the mustard seeds begin to pop. Add the vegetable mixture, and stir to combine.

Add the 3 cups of water, spice mix, turmeric, and salt, and bring to a boil. Turn the heat down to low and simmer, uncovered, for 25 minutes or longer, until the gravy is back to a salsa-like consistency.

Finish up the kofta balls while the gravy is simmering. Use a potato masher or fork to mash the mung beans well with the spice mix, pepper, ginger, and salt. If you press your hand into the dough, it should retain its shape and not fall apart or crumble. If it's too dry, add water, a tablespoon at a time, until you can form balls. Press 2 Tbsp of packed dough into your hands to make a ball, flattening them slightly into medallions. You should have enough dough to make about 20 balls.

Warm the ghee in a large, ceramic, nonstick frying pan on medium heat. Fry the balls in the ghee until browned on one side, about 3–5 minutes, then flip and brown the other side for about 2–3 minutes. Remove from the heat, and cover partially to keep the balls warm.

Spoon the finished gravy into 4 bowls, then place 4–5 kofta in each bowl, spooning additional gravy over the top. Garnish with fresh cilantro.

spiced pumpkin glee

SERVES 2 AS A MEAL OR 4 AS A SIDE

I think the recipe title should tell you how much I like pumpkin. This "dry curry" method is very common in Ayurvedic cookery. The vegetable may change with the seasons, and I encourage you to use this technique of a tempered sauté followed by a simmer to prepare whatever vegetables are on hand.

1 medium kabocha or similar winter squash

2 Tbsp coconut oil

1 tsp mustard seeds

1 tsp ground turmeric

1 tsp ground cinnamon

¼ cup shredded coconut

½ tsp freshly ground black pepper

1 cup water or broth

½ tsp salt (omit if using broth)

Wash the kabocha, halve it, and scoop out the seeds. Chop into 1-inch chunks, skin and all.

In a large frying pan, warm the coconut oil on medium heat. Add the mustard seeds, turmeric, cinnamon, coconut, and pepper to the oil, and sauté until the mustard seeds begin to pop. Add the kabocha, and stir until all pieces are coated with the oil. Continue to sauté and stir until the squash begins to stick to the pan, 2–4 minutes.

Add the water or broth and salt (if using); bring to a boil. Turn the heat down to medium-low and simmer, covered, until the pumpkin is soft, 20–25 minutes. If there is still a lot of liquid in the pan, then turn the heat up to medium-high for a couple of minutes to let most of it cook off. Most of the liquid should be gone.

Serve as a side with kichari or dal, or on its own as a light dinner.

Possible Pumpkin Problems

— ◆ ◆ ◆ —

Sadly, too much of a good thing is not indicated in the case of pumpkin and winter squashes in general. The combination of dry and dense qualities in these fiber-rich veggies, when taken in excess (in a body where heavy qualities already predominate) can clog the *srotas*. These channels transport liquids, wastes, nutrients, energy, and anything else that needs to move around. Keeping these channels clear for smooth transport is a key to optimum health. Luckily, when hearty winter squashes are taken in moderation (three to four times a week), they will nourish rather than clog our channels as we make it through winter.

creamy tahini kale

SERVES 2

This is an easy and delicious way to spruce up the usual kale. It is important to include some bitter vegetables in your diet, and this is one of my go-to dishes in cool weather. I always choose lacinato, or dinosaur, kale for its tenderness. Balance the light quality of leafy greens with the nutty depth of tahini. Enjoy this often in cool weather, alongside a soup or grain dish.

1 bunch lacinato kale, washed, stems removed, and torn into 2-inch pieces	2 Tbsp tahini
	Juice of ½ lemon
2 Tbsp water	Freshly ground black pepper to taste

Place the kale in a frying pan with 2 Tbsp water. Cover and steam on medium heat for 5 minutes, until kale is tender. Turn off the heat.

Mix the tahini and lemon juice in a small bowl. Pour the sauce over the steamed kale, and toss to coat each piece. Garnish with pepper.

cleansing kanjee

SERVES 4

Kanjee ("KAHN-ji") has as many forms as it does spellings. It is the absolute, all-the-time best healing food. Traditionally, and to this day, in Ayurveda clinics and hospitals, the digestion is nursed back to health with grain soup of increasing thickness as the patient begins to feels better. You don't have to be sick to eat it, and making this a healing part of your diet can ward off imbalances of all kinds.

10 cups water	¼ tsp each ground cumin,	**mix-ins (optional)**
1 cup brown basmati rice	turmeric, and ginger (or	Dates
¼ tsp salt	½ tsp Sweet Spice Mix)	Raisins

On high heat, bring water to a boil. In a large pot add rice, salt, and spices. Reduce heat to low and simmer, partially covered, for 1 hour, or until the rice breaks up and the soup appears creamy. Stir well before ladling into soup bowls.

Serve warm as a light meal or throughout the day to hydrate and nourish yourself when fasting.

When and How to Eat Kanjee

———— ◆ ◆ ◆ ————

Kanjee is easy to digest because the grain is watered down and well cooked. It can be used to hydrate, heal, and nourish the gut, as well as to restore balance to a lethargic dullness in the mind.

- *A light meal.* To lighten up, this dish can stand in for rice or bread and be served with cooked vegetable sides such as Creamy Tahini Kale (page 186) or Cumin Roasted Vegetables (page 170).
- *Hot breakfast.* Cook with dates, raisins, and Sweet Spice Mix for a hot breakfast cereal.
- *During stressful times.* In a period when stress is weakening your digestion but you still need to eat, kanjee is soothing and stabilizing.
- *A kanjee fast.* For weight loss or to sort out your gut after illness or indulgence, try a day-long kanjee fast, having as many bowls of it as you need to get through the day. This recipe should be enough for one day.

pickled beets

I eat pickled beets often, because they are so easy to make—and because the power of the beet pickle for healthy digestion cannot be underestimated! There are fancier, spicier pickles, but this recipe adds a digestive bit of sweet, sour, and salty to your meals in a jiffy with just a tablespoon or two. A bit of balsamic vinegar makes it even sweeter.

2 large or 3 medium beets (about 1½ lbs), without tops (to prepare tops, see Beet Coriander Soup on page 274)

1 Tbsp high-quality balsamic vinegar

2 Tbsp apple cider vinegar

½ tsp salt (optional)

In a large saucepan, bring enough water to a boil to cover the beets. Wash the beets and drop them into the water, untrimmed. Bring to a boil again on high heat. Cover, turn the heat down, and simmer until soft, 45–60 minutes. The time will depend on the size of your beets. Check softness with a fork or knife tip after 45 minutes.

Remove from the heat. Let the beets cool by submerging them in a bowl of cold water in your kitchen sink. When cool enough to touch, pour them into a colander to drain the water. Trim off the tops and tails. Under cold running water, slide the skins off the beets one by one. Slice the cooked beets into ¼-inch rounds, then make half-moons or ½-inch sticks.

Toss the beet pieces in a 16-oz glass jar with the vinegars and salt, if using. Stir before serving.

Refrigerate in a glass jar for up to 1 week.

carrot chutney

MAKES 2 CUPS

Carrots are an excellent choice for a sattvic diet. Sweet, slightly spicy, and simple, this chutney goes with most things. I am most likely to enjoy it alongside a rice or buckwheat dosa, with cashew rice, or on kichari. Omit the chili if you like, or split it and take the seeds out to reduce spiciness; the ginger will add some heat on its own. Going the extra mile to make the tempering is totally worth it! If you are keeping some of the chutney in the fridge, mix some of the tempered oil and spices into the leftover serving as well.

2 cups chopped carrots	1 tsp Sattvic Spice Mix	**tempering**
½ cup water	1-inch piece fresh ginger,	1 Tbsp coconut oil
1 dry red chili (optional)	peeled	1 tsp mustard seeds
1 tsp coconut oil	½ tsp salt	12 curry leaves (if you can
1 tsp fresh lemon juice		find them)

In a medium saucepan, steam the carrots in a steaming basket for 7–10 minutes. Set aside.

In a large frying pan over medium heat, sauté the whole chili (if using) and carrots in 1 tsp of coconut oil, stirring constantly, until they begin to brown slightly. Remove from the heat.

In a food processor or blender, grind all of the chutney ingredients together to a smooth paste. You will have to stop the blender and scrape down the sides a few times. Transfer to individual serving bowls.

In a small frying pan, heat the 1 Tbsp coconut oil on medium heat. Add the mustard seeds and curry leaves, and stir gently until they begin to pop. Cover the pan and fry for 1 minute. Remove from the heat, and pour the tempering over each chutney bowl.

Serve immediately alongside dosa, or use a large spoonful beside a rice dish.

Refrigerate in a glass container for up to 5 days. Allow to come to room temperature and stir well before serving.

miso tahini sauce

MAKES 1 CUP

Any fast-food place serving a "warm grain bowl" is bound to have a rich and creamy sauce like this one on the menu. You can recreate your own fresh and sattvic bowl at home in no time, complete with the digestive boost of lemon and pepper and the deep nutrition of good fats. Simply layer a grain, cooked vegetables, and a protein, and drizzle or toss with a few tablespoons of this sauce.

½ cup tahini	¼ cup olive oil	2 Tbsp warm water
2 Tbsp white miso	⅛ tsp freshly ground black	
¼ cup fresh lemon juice	pepper	

In a medium bowl, mix the tahini, miso, and lemon juice with a fork until they form a paste. Whisk in the olive oil and pepper until combined. Add the warm water and whisk. Add more warm water until the consistency is thin enough for drizzling.

Store, tightly covered, in a 16-oz glass jar. Shake vigorously before using. You can refrigerate it for 5–7 days.

"caramel"-dipped apples

MAKES ABOUT 2 CUPS

Dates have a special place in the Ayurvedic diet. While they can be heating and stimulating in large amounts, they also have an ability to nourish the deep tissues and are known as an aphrodisiac. They are a beneficial food for reproductive health—before and after pregnancy, and during lactation. This treat is for when you need a deep hit of sweetness, but keep in mind, it might just get you excited too.

10 fresh Medjool dates	1 tsp pure vanilla extract	2–4 apples, cored and
½ cup almond milk	Pinch of sea salt	sliced

Slice the dates in half and remove the pits. In a small bowl, soak the dates in the almond milk at room temperature for 1 hour. Pour the date and milk mixture into the blender, add the vanilla and salt, and blend until smooth. Serve alongside seasonal apple slices for dipping.

maple corn pudding

SERVES 4

This buttery but light dish is great for an autumnal dessert or breakfast. It is easy to prepare, naturally sweet, and simple to digest. Be sure to buy high-quality, organic cornmeal that is non-GMO, and balance the dry quality of the corn with a dose of ghee.

2 cups water	¼ tsp salt	1 Tbsp maple syrup,
½ cup coarse cornmeal	1 tsp ghee	for drizzling
1 tsp Sweet Spice Mix	¼ cup raisins	

Preheat oven to 350 degrees.

Bring the 2 cups of water to a boil in a teapot or saucepan. In a medium-size glass bowl, whisk together the cornmeal, Sweet Spice Mix, and salt. Take the water off the heat and pour over the cornmeal mixture. Add the ghee and whisk. Let stand for 15 minutes.

Evenly distribute the raisins in the bottom of 4 small ramekins. After the 15-minute standing time, stir the cornmeal mixture again and pour over the raisins in the ramekins. Bake for 20–25 minutes, until the edges are bubbly and the center is mostly firm and only slightly jiggly when you shake the ramekin.

Best enjoyed warm with a drizzle of maple syrup.

Trick or Treat

— ◆ ◆ ◆ —

I know what you're thinking. There sure are a lot of "treat" recipes in this cookbook. This is due to my personal love for creating sweet things and the love of sweet taste in the sattvic diet. Sweet taste, in moderation, is love and comfort. In excess, it is sloth and torpor. Take care to meditate on receiving the love as you enjoy the treats in this cookbook. Note how they are substantial, stand-alone recipes that will digest slowly and satisfy a true appetite as well as a sweet tooth. A smaller amount will satisfy if you pay attention and enjoy.

chocolate layered ojas bars

MAKES 20 SQUARES

Dates, pecans, almonds, and coconut are all foods known to support *ojas*, the nutrient cream of the body. This substance is our storehouse of deep energy and immunity, and it is a major player in building energy, long-term health, and stability of mind. Here, dense, naturally fatty foods combine with spices to ensure that your digestive fires are lit and the nutrition makes its way into the deep tissues of your body. These grounding ojas bars are an excellent way to replenish your energy supply if you are drained from too much activity.

base layer	chocolate layer	optional toppings
4 Medjool dates, pitted	½ cup coconut oil	2 Tbsp toasted coconut flakes
1 cup raw pecans	½ cup cacao powder	
½ cup raw almonds	3 Tbsp maple syrup	2 Tbsp chopped dried cranberries
2 Tbsp coconut oil		
¼ tsp salt		2 Tbsp sliced almonds
½ tsp Sweet Spice Mix		

Line the bottom of a 4 × 8-inch loaf pan with parchment paper.

In a food processor, pulse together the dates, pecans, almonds, 2 Tbsp coconut oil, salt, and Sweet Spice Mix until the mixture begins to stick together and form a ball. Press the date-nut mixture into the bottom of the pan.

Next, prepare one batch of Basic Coconut Chocolate (see page 143). Melt the coconut oil by standing the jar in hot water. In a small bowl, whisk together the ½ cup coconut oil, cacao, and maple syrup until smooth.

Working quickly, pour the chocolate coconut mixture over the base layer, tilting the pan from side to side so the chocolate is an even covering. Sprinkle with the topping of your choice (coconut flakes, dried cranberries, or slivered almonds). Place in the freezer for 30 minutes to 1 hour, until very firm.

Remove the loaf and parchment from the pan, and using a sharp knife on a cutting board, cut the frozen treat into small squares. Refrigerate the squares between layers of parchment paper in a sealed container for up to 14 days.

For a decadent treat, eat one square at a time and enjoy!

cacao-cranberry oat bars

MAKES 20 BARS

This is my winter go-to baking recipe. As the season goes on, I end up throwing all sorts of things in here—dates, almond meal, walnuts, orange zest. Oat bars are a meal and a great source of sustained energy. Top with fresh yogurt and a sprinkle of cinnamon for breakfast.

2½ cups rolled oats

½ cup Oat Flour

2 tsp Sweet Spice Mix

1 cup shredded coconut

1 cup applesauce

¼ cup maple syrup

1 cup coconut milk

¼ cup coconut oil

2 tsp pure vanilla extract

½ cup dried cranberries

½ cup cacao nibs

Preheat oven to 375 degrees. Grease a 9 × 13-inch glass baking dish with coconut oil.

Mix the oats, oat flour, spice mix, and coconut together in a large mixing bowl. Use a fork to beat the applesauce, maple syrup, coconut milk, ¼ cup coconut oil, and vanilla together in a medium bowl. Add the wet mixture to the dry ingredients, and stir just until combined. Fold in the cranberries and cacao nibs.

Spread the mixture evenly in the baking dish. Bake for 20–25 minutes, until edges just begin to brown. Do not overcook, or the bars will become dry. Remove from the oven and cool for 10 minutes before cutting.

Note: If you won't have help eating these, halve the recipe and use an 8-inch square pan.

Sugar-Free Cranberries

——— ◆ ◆ ◆ ———

Most dried cranberries are packaged with white sugar. They need a little sweetness to preserve nicely and not blow you away with sourness. There are, however, cranberries sweetened with apple juice concentrate, so look for these by reading the package ingredients. I only seem to find them in the bulk bins.

sesame date oat cakes

MAKES 12–15 CAKES

These cold-weather treats are a cross between a cookie and an oatcake. Oats, sesame, and dates are all a little bit unctuous and warming, providing grounding qualities that support a stable mind. They make a great breakfast with a cup of hot tea and travel well for a healthy, grounding snack.

1 Tbsp ground chia seeds	1 tsp Sweet Spice Mix	8 Medjool dates, pitted and
3 Tbsp water	1 cup tahini	diced
2 cups Oat Flour	3 Tbsp maple syrup	
¼ tsp coarse sea salt	1 tsp pure vanilla extract	

Preheat the oven to 325 degrees. Lightly grease a baking sheet with ghee or coconut oil. In a medium-size bowl, whisk together the chia seeds and water. Let stand for 5 minutes.

Place the oat flour, salt, and Sweet Spice Mix in a large mixing bowl.

To the chia seed mixture, add the tahini, maple syrup, and vanilla, and stir with a wooden spoon until smooth. Add the tahini mixture and dates to the flour, and stir until just combined.

Form 3 Tbsp of dough into a ball with your hands; place the balls 2 inches apart on the greased baking sheet. Continue until you run out of dough. With the palm of your hand, flatten each ball into a round medallion shape.

Bake 12–15 minutes, just until firm and slightly browned. Let cool 5–10 minutes before removing from the cookie sheet. Store in an airtight container at room temperature for up to 2 days.

yogi tea

SERVES 4

When I am overwhelmed, sometimes a cup of spicy, hot tea just brings everything down a notch. This is a great dairy-free alternative to traditional chai. It still has an authentic chai flavor and makes an exotic, aromatic, postmeal digestive that goes especially well alongside a dessert.

4 cups water

½ tsp ground cinnamon

1 tsp ground coriander

½-inch piece fresh ginger, cut into sticks

1 petal star anise (not a whole star)

½ tsp fennel seeds

2 Tbsp evaporated cane juice or coconut sugar

Combine all ingredients in a large saucepan, and bring to a boil on high heat. Reduce the heat and simmer, covered, for 15–20 minutes. Stir once as it's simmering to make sure the sweetener isn't stuck to the bottom.

Use a fine mesh strainer to strain the mixture into another saucepan or directly into mugs, and serve immediately.

herbal chai

Fans of masala chai can turn the stimulants down a notch by choosing this caffeine-free version. Traditionally, chai is made with fresh cow's milk, but if you can't get it or digest it, use one of the milk recipes in chapter 7. The spices in this recipe help you to digest the heavy qualities of cow's milk. For the most powerful medicinal effect, I call for whole spices boiled in the milk the old-school way, but in a pinch, you can use 2 tsp Sweet Spice Mix (see page 127).

1¼ cups milk (cow, almond, rice, or hemp seed)	1 Tbsp evaporated cane juice or coconut sugar	3–4 green cardamom pods, crushed
1 cup water	1-inch piece fresh ginger, crushed or chopped	½ tsp ground cinnamon

Combine all ingredients in a medium saucepan, and bring to a boil on high heat. Stay attentive, and reduce the heat before the milk begins to foam, or it will quickly boil over. Simmer, covered, for 10 minutes, or until your kitchen smells wonderful.

Take off the heat and use a fine mesh strainer to strain directly into two mugs to serve.

Milk note: Do not boil the hemp milk. Add it toward the end and heat until it is hot but not boiling.

honey rice shake

SERVES 2

Here is another warm, easy-to-digest smoothie recipe for you smoothie addicts out there. Brown rice and flaxseed provide some fiber for a satisfying drink, while the light, cleansing effects of honey sweeten without sitting heavily in your stomach.

½ cup cooked brown rice

2 Tbsp ground flaxseed
(optional)

1 tsp Sweet Spice Mix

2½ cups warm water

2 tsp raw honey

Combine the rice, flaxseeds (if using), spice mix, and warm water in a blender. Blend on high for 1 minute, opening the top to drop the honey into the blender while it is running, to avoid it sticking to the sides of the carafe.

Pour directly into two mugs, and serve warm.

all-healing turmeric milk

Also known as "golden milk," this evening tonic is well known in the Yoga and Ayurveda traditions for a long list of benefits, namely as an anti-inflammatory, bone nourisher, and immune booster. This synergistic combination of turmeric, coconut, ginger, and pepper is supported by ancient knowledge and by modern research as well. You will find it not only healing, but comforting. If you think drinking an entire cup of milk, even warm and spiced, is a bit heavy, use half milk and half water.

1 cup whole cow's milk or almond milk

1 tsp ground turmeric

½ tsp ground ginger

1 tsp coconut oil

Pinch of freshly ground black pepper

½–1 tsp raw honey (optional)

In a small saucepan, warm the milk uncovered over medium-high heat for 2–4 minutes, or until you see steam rising out of the pan. Add all the other ingredients, except the honey, and whisk by hand or with an immersion blender until combined.

Pour into a mug, sweeten with honey (if using), and drink immediately.

Sleep or Death

⸺ ◆ ◆ ◆ ⸺

Ayurveda tells us that life and death are dependent upon sleep! Well, when you put it that way, why not go to bed a little earlier? The generally recommended bedtime is no later than 10 P.M. After that, the body gets a second wind, and the energy that is meant to detoxify the body during sleep goes to external pursuits. The problem with skipping lunch and eating a big dinner is that it will disturb your sleep and cause you to stay up later. On an evening when you get home too late for a meal or have a light appetite, have this golden milk—or a warm Honey Rice Shake (page 201) for vegans—and go to bed.

lassi

SERVES 1

This is nothing like a restaurant lassi. In India, it is known as buttermilk, or *takra*, but outside of India, "buttermilk" can mean the store-bought version, which does not have the same qualities or health benefits. The traditional process of churning to remove fats changes the heavy qualities to light. This digestive can be used 30 minutes before a meal to improve your appetite or following a meal to reduce indigestion and bloating. Be sure to make it fresh for the medicinal benefit.

1 cup water, room temperature	¼ cup whole-milk yogurt Dash of ground turmeric	Double dash of ground ginger

Put the water in a 16-oz glass jar, and add the yogurt and spices. Churn the mixture on high speed for 1 minute with an immersion hand blender, or in a high-speed blender, until it foams. The milk solids will gather on top and stick to the sides of the jar; they look like little bubbles. Skim off the solids with a spoon and discard. Repeat until there are no more fats to remove.

Drink immediately.

agni boost:

Increase a sluggish digestive fire by adding ¼ tsp each of freshly ground black pepper and ground cumin to this lassi and taking it before meals, one to three times daily until your appetite improves.

9

recipes *to* relax *and* calm rajas

rajas

— ◆ ◆ ◆ —

Rajas is the energy of manifestation. This passionate, creative drive makes stuff happen and brings a warrior spirit to any endeavor. Its excitable nature can have an all-or-nothing approach. What a rajasic minds needs is a little moderation. If you find yourself feeling over-worked, irritated, or agitated, the foods in this section will help you relax, cool your jets, and restore a state of balance in which things still get done, but your mind is not *overly* active. These recipes are tasty without being overly spicy and offer satisfying replacements for go-to spicy, salty, and oily foods. Rejuvenate with fresh greens and juicy fruits; harmonize with mellow mint and almond; and spice it up with exotic, yet calming tastes like cardamom and coconut.

calming rajas

———— ◆ ◆ ◆ ————

Rajas feels like:
restless, overworked, overstimulated, irritable,
anxious, inconsistent, too busy, trouble sleeping

Potential Signs and Symptoms of Imbalance

- Acid stomach
- Overheating
- Tension headaches
- Difficulty falling asleep or waking up
  in the wee hours
- Racing thoughts
- Irritability/reactivity
- Inability to sit still
- Attachment to work, media devices, Internet, and TV
- Tendency to be overly competitive
  or critical

Tastes to Enjoy
Sweet, bitter, astringent

Foods to Favor
Coconut (oil, water, milk, sugar, and meat)
Fresh, seasonal vegetables, especially
    cucumber, zucchini, fennel, and watercress
Small beans (lentils, mung, adzuki, black, and red)
Sweet, juicy seasonal fruits, especially grapes and melons
Fresh herbs, especially parsley and cilantro

Foods to Reduce

Ferments

Kombucha

Unripe or sour fruits

Sour cream

Stinky cheeses

Red meat

Eggs, especially the yolks

Onions

Garlic

Vinegar

Salty condiments

Alcohol

Coffee and caffeine

Chocolate

Chili peppers

Restaurant food

Chips, crackers, and popcorn

Stimulants

Smoking

General Lifestyle Guidelines

Avoid overexercising.

Get enough sleep.

Get to bed by 10 P.M.

Nap occasionally if needed.

Eat regular, sit-down meals.

Eat snack foods and restaurant foods sparingly.

Take time to prepare and enjoy meals.

Schedule me-time.

Allow for quiet time and outdoor time.

baked buckwheat
with cardamom and blueberries

SERVES 3–4

This hearty breakfast is a bit warming and best for cold weather and active mornings. The cleansing action of the blueberries and the cool taste of the cardamom and almond milk combine to make a grain-free, powerhouse morning meal that will keep you satisfied until lunch. The best part is that a warm square in a sealed container will go with you anywhere. You can also revisit the pan at day's end for a simple dinner.

2 Tbsp coconut oil, melted, plus extra for greasing the pan

1½ cups buckwheat groats

1 tsp ground cardamom

1 tsp baking powder

¼ tsp salt

3 cups almond milk, plus extra for serving

1 tsp pure vanilla extract

¼ cup maple syrup

1½ cups blueberries

Preheat oven to 350 degrees. Prepare a 8-inch square glass baking dish by greasing with coconut oil.

Pulse the buckwheat groats in a food processor or high-speed blender until coarsely broken/chopped. The goal is not to make a flour, but rather to have a coarse buckwheat meal, with some groats split in half while others remain fully intact.

In a medium bowl, combine the chopped groats, cardamom, baking powder, and salt. Add the almond milk, vanilla, coconut oil, and maple syrup; stir to combine. Pour the mixture into the prepared baking dish, and top with the blueberries.

Bake, uncovered, for 45–50 minutes, until slightly browned. Remove from the oven, and allow to cool for 10 minutes before serving. Spoon into dishes, and drizzle with maple syrup and additional almond milk. Refrigerate up to 3 days in an airtight container.

coconut chia seed pudding

SERVES 2

Ayurveda is very specific about eating honey only when it is raw. When boiled, honey becomes a thick sludge the body can't digest. Yet raw honey has a special "scraping" ability that can be used to detoxify the body. That's my kind of sweetener! Therefore, I dream up recipes that can be sweetened with honey without heating it. Here's one.

1½ cups coconut milk	1 Tbsp raw honey	¼ tsp ground ginger
⅓ cup chia seeds	1 tsp pure vanilla extract	

In a small bowl, whisk together the coconut milk and chia seeds. Stir in the honey, vanilla, and ginger. Pour into two serving bowls or small jelly jars, and let sit for 30 minutes to 1 hour. If you're making it the day before, keep it in the refrigerator, and set out on the counter for 1 hour before eating to allow the pudding to return to room temperature.

A Word on Patience

◆ ◆ ◆

According to the Charaka Samhita, patience is the key to managing the mind. Culturally, the modern world is quite concerned with timeliness and productivity, both goals that—if not coupled with patience—lead to mental agitation. The morning is an ideal time to contemplate patience, as the whole day still lies ahead. The energy with which the day begins, be it contentment, restlessness, or lethargy, inevitably carries over into the day. Setting aside nonnegotiable time for morning rituals and breakfast will set the tone and encourage a life of balance. Check out chapter 5 for some morning practice ideas (see page 98).

apple raisin breakfast kichari

SERVES 3–4

This kichari is a protein-rich oatmeal replacement. When the apples start coming by the bushel, I cook them right in with my staple food as a breakfast cereal. It doesn't have to be morning to eat it if you are in the mood for a sweet, satisfying hot meal.

½ cup basmati rice

½ cup yellow split mung beans, soaked overnight or at least a few hours

4 cups water

2 tsp ground cinnamon or Sweet Spice Mix

¼ cup raisins

2 apples, cored and chopped into ½-inch cubes

1½ Tbsp maple syrup

1 Tbsp ghee

½ tsp salt

Rinse the rice and dal well. In a medium saucepan, bring the water to a boil on high heat. Add the rinsed rice and dal to the boiling water. Turn the heat down and simmer, uncovered, for 15–20 minutes.

Add the cinnamon, raisins, apples, and maple syrup. Cover and simmer 15–20 minutes more, adding more water if needed. Go for the consistency of thick oatmeal.

Turn off the heat and stir in the ghee and salt. Let stand for 5 minutes before eating (if you can).

Hot Meal

◆ ◆ ◆

I remember in grammar school signing up for a "hot meal" at lunchtime. The natural intelligence of craving a hot meal is something to listen to. There are times when the day is moving too fast, and I know I need to have a sit-down, hot meal to get steady and sustain my mental energy for the day. I have learned, over time, that I will pay the price by week's end if I compromise on the midday meal. Prepare a thermos if you are on the go, and prioritize the time you need to sit down for that hot meal.

sprouted greens soup

SERVES 2

The sprouted beans add a live protein, but you would never know they were in there when you are enjoying this creamy, sweet soup. You get full bang for your buck by sitting down to enjoy this nutritious dish, absolutely packed with bitter, sweet, and astringent vegetables. It's a great antidote to overindulgence. If you don't like the licorice taste of fennel, leave it out, double the parsley, and add a handful of Swiss chard or spinach.

2 cups vegetable broth

½ cup Sprouted Mung
 Beans

1 cup chopped green beans

½ fennel root, cored, ends
 trimmed, and sliced into
 ½-inch chunks

1 tsp Calming Spice Mix

½ cup parsley leaves

2 tsp coconut oil

In a medium saucepan, bring 1 cup of the broth to a boil on high heat. Add the mung beans, green beans, fennel, and spice mix. Lower the heat and simmer, covered, for 5–10 minutes. A longer simmer will yield a creamier soup.

Transfer the vegetables and broth to a blender, and add the parsley, oil, and the rest of the broth. Puree until smooth. (If using an immersion blender, add parsley, oil, and remaining broth to the saucepan and blend until smooth.)

Serve with a rice or buckwheat dosa.

Green Soup Cleansing Reaction

— ◆ ◆ ◆ —

This soup is incredibly cleansing and can speed up your digestion. If your diet does not include a lot of greens and legumes generally, start with a small bowl as an accompaniment to other foods, like a grain dish or baked sweet potato, rather than a large bowl as an entree.

calming kichari

SERVES 4-6

This is a classic dish that grounds you, calms you, and sustains you all at the same time. I've added the healthy bitterness of greens to cooling herbs and spices to mellow the mental heat of a busy day. When you feel like your mind is orbiting a bunch of tasks or appointments, have a leisurely sit-down with a bowl of this, and I guarantee you will feel calmer.

6 cups water	2 cups kale, Swiss chard,	**tempering**
1 cup basmati rice	or collards, coarsely	1–2 Tbsp ghee
½ cup yellow split mung	chopped into strips	½ tsp cumin seeds
beans, soaked overnight	½–1 tsp salt	½ tsp coriander seeds
or at least a few hours	½ cup fresh cilantro leaves,	½ tsp fennel seeds
1 Tbsp Calming Spice Mix	for garnish	(optional)

In a large saucepan, boil 5 cups of the water on high heat. Set the other cup aside to add during cooking as needed.

Rinse the rice and dal twice or until water runs clear. Add them to the boiling water, along with the spice mix, and keep on high heat until the liquid boils again. Immediately turn the heat down and simmer, partially covered, for 20 minutes without stirring. Check after 20 minutes to see if the dal is submerged. If not, pour the additional cup of water on top but do not stir. Place the greens on top to steam. Simmer, partially covered, 10 minutes more.

To make the tempering, warm the ghee in a small skillet on medium heat. Add the cumin, coriander, and fennel seeds (if using), and cook until the seeds pop, about 2–3 minutes. Remove from the heat, and pour into the kichari. Add the salt, stir well, and let stand, covered, for a few minutes.

Kichari should have a soupy, soft consistency. Serve it in bowls, as you would a stew. Garnish with lots of fresh cilantro.

your daily dal

This soup is an absolute protein staple. The colorful yet simple nature of such a meal, enjoyed quietly, is sure to please the senses, ground the body, and mellow agitation. The thing about rajas is how much the mind *moves*, and that mental exercise makes you hungry for stabilizing foods like protein. A traditional Ayurvedic *thali* meal will include this yellow dal seasoned with ghee-sautéed cumin seeds. I eat this often, usually adding a pile of steamed greens drizzled with an extra teaspoon of oil and a pickle or chutney, sometimes a dosa. It's so good!

---

6 cups water

1 cup yellow split mung beans, soaked overnight or at least a few hours

1 tsp ground turmeric

1 tsp ground coriander

1 Tbsp Calming Spice Mix

6 medium carrots, coarsely chopped (about 2 cups)

½ tsp salt, plus more to taste

2 tsp coconut oil

1 tsp cumin seeds

Small handful of curry leaves (12–15 leaves, fresh or frozen if necessary)

Juice of ½ lime

2 Tbsp chopped cilantro, for garnish (optional)

In a large saucepan, heat 4 cups of the water to a boil on high heat. While the water is heating, rinse the split mung beans in cool water until the water runs clear. Add the beans, turmeric, coriander, and spice mix to the saucepan. Turn the heat down to low and simmer, partially covered, for 20 minutes.

Add the carrots to the pot and bring the water to a boil again. Add the remaining 2 cups of water and the salt; no need to stir. Simmer, partially covered, for another 10 minutes.

In a small frying pan, heat the coconut oil over medium heat. Add the cumin seeds and curry leaves, and sauté until you can smell the spices, about 2–3 minutes. Add the tempered spices to the dal for the last 5 minutes of the cooking time. Remove from the heat, and stir in the lime juice.

Serve in bowls with a topping of the fresh cilantro or with a lime wedge.

Note: If your dal is not as creamy as you would like, soften the beans by blending the hot dal with an immersion hand blender or an old-fashioned eggbeater for 5–10 seconds before you add the vegetables. Alternatively, soak the beans overnight before cooking, and they will soften quickly.

butternut squash soup

SERVES 4

If you are around the house for an hour in the fall or winter, why not roast a squash? The beautiful smell will fill your home and bring a cozy, grounding feeling to your cooking space. Just stick the squash in the oven whole while you do your thing, come back in an hour, scoop it out, and make a soup in 15 minutes.

1 butternut squash	1 tsp ground cinnamon	Salt and freshly ground
2 medium apples	¼ tsp ground cloves	black pepper to taste
2 Tbsp ghee or coconut oil	1 tsp ground cumin	½ cup coconut milk
1-inch piece fresh ginger,	3 cups vegetable broth	
peeled and chopped	½ tsp ground turmeric	

To roast the squash, place upright on a baking sheet and roast at 400 degrees for 1–1½ hours, until tender. Cut the roasted squash in half, scoop out the seeds, peel, and cut into large pieces.

Peel and chop the apples into 1-inch pieces. Heat the ghee or coconut oil in a large, heavy-bottomed saucepan. Add the apples, chopped ginger, cinnamon, cloves, and cumin. Sauté, stirring occasionally, until the apples soften and the spices are fragrant, about 7 minutes. Add the broth, roasted squash, turmeric, and salt and pepper to the pot. Bring to a boil, then turn the heat down and simmer, uncovered, for 10 minutes. Remove from the heat, add the coconut milk, and blend with a hand blender.

You Are *Not* Too Busy to Make Soup!

— ◆ ◆ ◆ —

I'm astounded by how complicated soup recipes can be. All the different steps, standing there stirring . . . I'd rather cook it and blend it. Done. If you are overworked and stressed, you need a bowl of hot soup. There's no need to devote an hour or more to the task. My soup recipes are so easy, you will be nurturing yourself with these comfort foods in no time.

coconut-lime baked sweet potatoes

SERVES 2–4

These twice-baked sweet potatoes are divine and a feast for the eyes. They are easy to make and offer a calming mixture of digestive spices, along with the smooth, sweet taste of sweet potato and coconut milk. Serve them open-faced, sprinkled with cilantro and mustard seed.

2 medium sweet potatoes

2 Tbsp coconut oil, plus extra for rubbing on potato skins before baking

¼ cup full-fat coconut milk

Juice of ½ lime

½ tsp ground coriander

½ tsp ground turmeric

¼ tsp black mustard seeds

¼ tsp coarse sea salt

2 Tbsp fresh cilantro, roughly chopped

Preheat oven to 350 degrees. Prick the potatoes a few times with a fork. Rub coconut oil over the skins. Place on a rimmed baking sheet, and bake for 50–60 minutes, or until soft. Remove from the oven and allow to cool until you can handle them.

Cut each sweet potato in half lengthwise and scoop out the insides, leaving a ¼-inch shell on all sides. Place the skins back on the baking tray and set aside. Transfer the inside flesh to a food processer or mixing bowl. Add the coconut oil, coconut milk, lime juice, coriander, and turmeric. Pulse or stir just until smooth. Divide the sweet potato filling among the four skins.

Return the stuffed sweet potatoes to the oven and bake for 10 minutes, then turn the oven to broil and crisp the tops for 2–3 minutes. Remove from the oven and garnish with mustard seeds, sea salt, and cilantro.

mixed market vegetables
with herbed yogurt sauce

SERVES 2

This summertime favorite is easy to prepare, and you can feel free to use whatever vegetables and fresh herbs are available—this is my favorite combo. I go for a fine mixture of colors and change the herb each time. The sauce is quick enough to make fresh to order. This vegetable side goes nicely with a dal soup.

2 small carrots	2 Tbsp water	Freshly ground pepper to
1 medium zucchini	½ tsp salt	taste
1 medium summer squash	½ cup Fresh Yogurt	2 Tbsp fresh herbs, finely
1 Tbsp ghee	Juice of ½ lime	chopped (basil, dill,
½ tsp cumin seeds	¼ tsp Calming Spice Mix	oregano, cilantro, parsley,
½ cup fresh peas or	¼ tsp salt	etc.)
green beans		

Chop the squashes and carrots into 1-inch chunks.

In a large frying pan, warm the ghee on medium heat. Sauté the cumin seeds until you can smell them, 3–5 minutes. Add the squashes, carrots, and peas, and stir to coat. Sauté for a few minutes.

Keeping the stovetop on medium heat, add the water and salt. Cover and steam until tender, about 10 minutes. Test vegetables by pricking them with a fork. If the fork enters the vegetables easily, they are done. Remove from the heat, uncover, and cool for a few minutes. If there is any water left in the pan, pour it into a bowl to save for the yogurt sauce (if needed).

Toss the vegetables with the yogurt sauce in a serving bowl. Garnish with fresh herbs.

For the yogurt sauce:
Whisk the yogurt, lime juice, spice mix, salt, and pepper together to combine. Add 1–2 Tbsp of the leftover cooking water if your sauce is very thick. This will depend on the yogurt you are using. Add the herbs, setting a small amount aside for garnish.

Vegan variation:
Substitute full-fat coconut milk for the yogurt.

maple oven-roasted fennel with cinnamon

SERVES 4-6

Something gently sweet on the plate rounds out the six tastes in a meal for a true sattvic experience. The caramelizing of fennel's natural sugar with maple syrup and browned to perfection is pleasing for the eye and the palate. I like to serve Hearty French Lentil Kichari in a wide bowl, with three or four slices of this fennel layered on top.

4 fennel bulbs

2 Tbsp maple syrup

1 Tbsp coconut oil, melted

½ tsp ground cinnamon

¼ tsp salt

Preheat oven to 425 degrees. Line 2 baking sheets with parchment paper.

Leave 2 inches of the stem on top of the fennel bulbs (for appearance), and slice the fennel lengthwise into ⅓-inch slices.

Mix the maple syrup, coconut oil, cinnamon, and salt together in a small bowl. Brush the fennel slices on both sides with the maple mixture. Arrange the slices in single layers on the baking sheets.

Bake for 8–10 minutes, until the fennel begins to brown. Remove from the oven and flip the slices. Bake for an additional 8–10 minutes, until browned and caramelized.

Serve immediately.

Fantastic Fennel

— ◆ —

The fennel plant has a host of health benefits recognized by Ayurveda and Western science alike. The fresh bulb and dried seeds are featured in home remedies in its native Europe. Enjoy the cooling, digestive, anti-inflammatory properties of this plant, which is a relative of parsley. It relieves bloating and acid stomach and freshens breath! The only reason not to cook with fennel is if you don't like its licorice taste.

farmers' market rice noodle bowl

SERVES 2 AS A MEAL OR 4 AS A SIDE

This miso soup is chock-full of colorful late summer vegetables and the golden goodness of ghee. You'll be surprised how quick it is to create an authentic tasting noodle bowl at home, without being tempted by sugary, spicy condiments like oyster sauce and hot sauce—both of which contain cornstarch, white sugar, and artificial flavorings. Enjoy with a large spoon and chopsticks, and watch your shirt!

2 Tbsp ghee

½ cup julienned carrots

1 medium zucchini, sliced and cut into half-moons

1 bunch baby bok choy, sliced into ribbons

½ cup sliced radishes

2-inch piece fresh ginger, peeled and chopped

2 Tbsp tamari, plus more to taste

4 cups water, plus ¼ cup hot water for miso paste

One 8-oz package thin rice noodles

1 Tbsp miso paste

2 Tbsp chopped cilantro

½ lime, cut into wedges for serving

In a heavy-bottomed saucepan, melt the ghee over medium-high heat. Add the carrots, zucchini, bok choy, and radishes, and sauté for 5–8 minutes, stirring occasionally. When the vegetables have softened, add the ginger and tamari, and sauté for another minute, stirring constantly. Add the water, scraping the spices and seasoning from the bottom of the pan, and bring to a boil. Turn down the heat, and simmer for 10 minutes. After simmering, remove the pan from the heat, add the rice noodles, cover, and let sit for 5 minutes.

Meanwhile, in a small bowl, dissolve the miso paste in ¼ cup of hot water. Add the miso to the saucepan and stir. Using tongs, distribute the veggies and noodles into individual serving bowls, then ladle the broth on top. Garnish with cilantro, fresh lime wedges, and additional tamari if desired.

Note: Make it a meal by adding one block of firm tofu, chopped into ½-inch cubes, when you add the water.

quick buckwheat dosa
with mint chutney

SERVES 2–3 (6–8 DOSAS)

Dosa batters are traditionally fermented at home to assist digestion, and they add a scintillating sour taste. This recipe is for a "quick dosa batter," where the sour taste comes from yogurt, and the batter is ready to use after just 10 minutes. As we all get busier and busier, a quick batter can be a real life-saver. Buckwheat is slower to digest than white rice or wheat batters, so it will stick to your ribs—in a good way—and keep you satisfied until your next meal. I often serve this as a breakfast food; I keep the batter in the refrigerator for a few days so I can have it anytime.

Serve it with Mint Chutney (recipe follows) and a quick pickle to get your six tastes.

QUICK BUCKWHEAT DOSA

1 cup buckwheat flour	½ tsp Vitalizing Spice Mix	¾ cup water
½ cup whole-milk yogurt	½ tsp salt	1 Tbsp ghee or coconut oil

Mix the buckwheat flour, yogurt, spice mix, and salt together until smooth. Add the water, a tablespoon at a time, until the consistency becomes like pancake batter. Let stand for 10 minutes.

Heat a ceramic, nonstick fry pan on medium-high heat. The pan is ready when you flick water on it and it sizzles immediately. Add 1 tsp of the ghee to the pan. Ladle about ½ cup of the batter onto the pan, and spread out to a very thin circle by tipping the pan or using the back of a large spoon. Fill in any spaces with extra batter. If you are having a hard time spreading the batter, add more water—again, by the tablespoon—to thin the mixture.

Cook until the batter begins to firm and appear dry, about 3–4 minutes. Flip, and brown the other side for about 1 minute. Continue making dosas until you have used up all the batter. If the batter starts to stick, add an additional teaspoon of ghee to the pan.

Serve immediately.

MINT CHUTNEY

MAKES 1 CUP

Mint chutney just doesn't come out well without a little chili. Luckily the cooling, calming attributes of fresh mint balance out the heat. Take the seeds out of the chili first to ensure you don't get zapped. This is a great way to use up those plentiful bunches of mint in the summer. Serve it with dosa or grain dishes.

1½ cups packed fresh mint leaves

1 cup packed fresh cilantro leaves

Juice of ½ lime

2 Tbsp water

½ cup unsweetened, dried coconut

1 serrano chili, deseeded

1 tsp Vitalizing Spice Mix

Salt to taste

In a food processor or blender, blend the mint, cilantro, lime juice, and water until coarsely chopped. Add the rest of the ingredients and blend until smooth, adding a tablespoon of water at a time, if needed, to process.

Store covered in the refrigerator for up to 1 week.

coconut and cashew rice pulao

SERVES 3–4

Preparing this dish will transport you to southern India as you sauté the whole spices, releasing their aromatic qualities into your kitchen. Have a great trip! *Pulao* ("PUHL-ow") is mentioned in ancient texts, and this pilaf-style dish is lighter than its rajasic counterpart *biryani*, which tends to be very spicy and nonvegetarian. Keep it sattvic, yet exotic, by using cardamon pods and curry leaves instead of lots of chilies and onions.

- 1 cup basmati rice, soaked 20–30 minutes in 2 cups water
- 2 Tbsp coconut oil
- 1 tsp mustard seeds
- 2–3 green cardamom pods, cracked
- 1-inch piece fresh ginger, peeled and chopped into matchsticks
- 1 Tbsp Calming Spice Mix
- 6 curry leaves (optional)
- 1 cup mixed seasonal vegetables, chopped into
- bite-size pieces (Peas, carrots, and green beans are good here.)
- ¼ cup cashew halves
- 1 cup coconut milk
- 1 cup water
- 1 tsp salt

Drain and rinse the rice until the water runs clear. Set aside.

Warm the oil in a large saucepan or wok on medium heat. Add the mustard seeds, cardamom pods, ginger, spice mix, and curry leaves (if using). Stir until the mustard seeds begin to pop. Add the vegetables and stir until coated. Stir in the cashews and sauté for 1 minute. Add the rice grains and stir until coated. Stir in the coconut milk, water, and salt. Cover and simmer on low heat for 20 minutes.

Take off the heat. Uncover and fluff with a fork; cover for 5 more minutes if all the liquid is not absorbed. Pull out the cardamom pods if you see them.

Serve with Mint Chutney or Vegetable Cilantro Raita.

Cooking with Green Cardamom Pods

— ◆ ◆ ◆ —

I've developed a few methods for cracking the green pods; some are better than others. I used to crush them with the back of a serving spoon or a knife, which sent the little black seeds inside spinning. They are too expensive to lose behind the dish rack. Now, I crack each pod gently with my teeth and toss them in one by one. If I have guests, I crush them quickly in a mortar and pestle. (The pods, not the guests.) You only need to crack cardamom pods so the cooking juices can get in; don't allow the seeds to escape into the dish.

roasted cauliflower kale salad

SERVES 2

The creation of this warm salad at home will transport you to a bistro, much like the one in New York City that inspired this recipe. That one had cheese and garlic on it, which I have replaced with tahini and hemp seeds, for a rajas-relieving version. What a nice way to eat cauliflower and kale!

1 small head cauliflower, chopped into small florets (about 5 cups)	2 Tbsp ghee, melted	Juice of ½ lemon
	1 bunch kale, destemmed and chopped into small pieces (about 4 cups)	1 Tbsp hemp seeds
1 tsp ground turmeric		1 tsp freshly ground black pepper
½ tsp salt	2 Tbsp olive oil	2 Tbsp tahini

Preheat oven to 350 degrees.

Place the cauliflower in a mixing bowl, sprinkle with the turmeric and the salt, then toss with melted ghee. Transfer to a baking dish and roast for 25–30 minutes, tossing once after about 12 minutes. Remove from the oven when the florets are lightly browned.

Place the kale in the same mixing bowl, and drizzle with olive oil and lemon juice. Massage the oil and juice into the kale until coated; the leaves should begin to soften. Let stand for 10 minutes or longer to soften to taste. If in doubt, massage the oil more vigorously into the kale, and let stand for a full 30 minutes.

Add the warm cauliflower, hemp seeds, and pepper to the kale. Toss. Transfer the mixture to serving bowls, and drizzle each bowl with tahini. Serve warm.

Kale note: Substitute baby kale if you'd like to cut out the massaging step and eat sooner.

Brain Food

◆ ◆ ◆

In Ayurveda, as well as in other indigenous health systems, plants that resemble certain organs are known to be nourishing for those tissues, such as kidney beans for adrenal health or walnuts and cauliflower for the brain. Take note of how a head of cauliflower looks very much like a brain; it's no wonder this vegetable is considered brain food.

vegetable cilantro raita

This colorful side dish contains all six tastes. This sattvic take on the classic dish leaves out the raw onion but still pairs beautifully with spicy foods to balance heat and offer a digestive boost of probiotics. Homemade yogurt, which is sweet as well as gently sour, accompanied by bitter and pungent spices and a bit of astringency from vegetables, will complete any sattvic meal. Serve this alongside rice dishes, dals, and cooked vegetables.

1 cup Fresh Yogurt	1 carrot	½ tsp mustard seeds
¼ cup water	½ tsp salt	½ tsp cumin seeds
½ cucumber, peeled and deseeded	¼ cup chopped cilantro	¼ tsp ground turmeric
	1 tsp ghee	

Whisk the yogurt and water together. Grate the cucumber and the carrot. Mix into the yogurt, along with the salt and cilantro.

Warm the ghee in a small frying pan over medium heat. Add the mustard seeds, cumin seeds, and ground turmeric. Sauté until the mustard seeds begin to pop and you can smell the spices. Take off the heat immediately. Pour into the yogurt mixture, and stir until combined.

This is fabulous served with rice dishes or on a bed of greens. It will keep in the fridge for up to 5 days.

The Skinny on Salt

— ◆ ◆ ◆ —

While we are on the topic of condiments, salt is an important player. Salty taste heats the body due to the presence of the fire element in its composition, which is important in cold weather. Salt's hydrating effect also calms the nervous system by softening and relaxing the body. Not all salt is created equal, however. Table salt is demineralized, which removes its therapeutic effects. Sea salt has large molecules that are hard to digest, while pink salt has smaller molecules and bio-available minerals. Ayurveda has long favored pink salt, and it's all I use in my cooking. Its modern trade name is Himalayan pink salt, and it's easy to find.

almond cilantro chutney

MAKES ABOUT 1½ CUPS

This chutney showcases a host of fresh, cooling ingredients to provide a good dose of balance when the heat is on. Almond, lime, and cilantro together are not only creamy and delicious, but also incredibly bright and refreshing. Cilantro is known for its cooling, relaxing effect on the body. Try a big spoonful of this chutney alongside a grain dish, vegetables, and especially Coconut and Cashew Rice Pulao (see page 233) to add color and calm. When you are entertaining, you will find it's a crowd pleaser with crackers.

1 bunch fresh cilantro	½ cup raw almonds, soaked	½ tsp ground coriander
¼ cup fresh lime juice	in water for at least 1 hour	1 tsp maple syrup (optional)
(about 1½ limes)	(measure before soaking)	½ tsp salt
2 Tbsp water	2 Tbsp fresh ginger,	¼ tsp freshly ground black
	chopped	pepper

Cut the bottom 2 inches off the cilantro and wash. In a food processor or blender, blend the lime juice, water, and cilantro until the cilantro is coarsely chopped.

If using a food processor, add the rest of the ingredients and blend until smooth. If using a blender, you may need to pour the cilantro paste into a bowl, and put the almonds in the bottom of the blender. Place the paste on top and pulse to blend until smooth, adding a tablespoon of water at a time, if needed, to process.

Store covered in the refrigerator for up to 1 week.

peach blueberry cobbler

SERVES 4

When the summer fruits are ripe, there is no combo I like more than peaches and blueberries. A bit of sour taste from peaches brightens this dessert, while blueberries balance the summer heat. The addition of almond meal, coconut oil, and digestive spices make for a healthy, nutritious treat that won't weigh you down.

¼ cup coconut oil, melted, plus extra for greasing the dish

2 cups fresh blueberries (Buy a quart and have plenty to nibble on.)

3 peaches, diced into 1-inch pieces

1 cup almond meal

½ cup oats

2 Tbsp coconut sugar

1 tsp ground ginger

¼ tsp salt

1 tsp pure vanilla extract

Preheat oven to 350 degrees. Grease an 8-inch square baking dish with coconut oil. Place the blueberries and peaches in the greased baking dish.

In a mixing bowl, use a fork to combine the almond meal, oats, coconut sugar, ginger, and salt, breaking up any clumps as you go. Add the coconut oil and vanilla, and mix until just combined. Crumble the almond and oat topping evenly over the fruit.

Bake 35–45 minutes, or until the fruit is bubbly and the topping begins to brown. Serve warm.

Note: You can certainly double this recipe and use a 9 × 13-inch pan. Your cooking time may vary.

steamed plantains

SERVES 2

This is the easiest warm after-school snack ever—a comfort food to relax the system. A variety of plantain, known in southern India as "Kerala banana," is often sliced, dried, and fried in coconut oil to be served at special meals. A sattvic take on this celebration staple is to omit the frying and steam the plantain. Make sure you begin with a ripe plantain. I always find plantains at Latin and Indian markets.

1 large ripe plantain

½ cup water

Slice off the stem of the plantain. Leaving the skin on, slice into 1-inch pieces. Stand the pieces side by side in a steamer basket. Place the basket over the ½ cup of water in a medium saucepan. Bring the water to a boil on high heat, then turn the heat down to medium and simmer for 10 minutes. Remove from the heat.

Use an oven mitt to pull the steamer out and pour the plantain chunks onto a plate. Allow to cool for a few minutes, until they can be handled. Serve with the skin on, and gently pull the skin until it tears lengthwise. Enjoy the hot plantain right out of the skin.

Desire

The body is an instrument of the mind. The sense organs are really running the show—our untrained senses have us running around with these desires to taste, touch, smell, purchase, procreate! The senses fill the mind, and the mind keeps sending the body on the errands of the senses. We keep eating and buying and talking. Meanwhile, modernity has created super-sense temptations, like white sugar, "fragrance," IMAX movie theaters, and subwoofers. SOS! Slow it down, relax, and allow your senses to adjust to a bit of quiet. You can start with a simple, sweet treat like these plantains, instead of taking a ride on the cookie express. (For more on taking care of your senses, see chapter 5.)

bombay carrot halwa

SERVES 4-6

This ubiquitous dessert is served all over India at holidays and fancy meals. I call it Bombay Halwa because the sweet shop in Mysore, a city where I spend a good deal of time, is called Bombay Tiffany's. Although it's often made with condensed milk, I've toned down the fats and sugars for this sattvic version—it still smells and tastes aaah-mazing, and it brings the cooling benefits of almonds. Be sure to warn your guests to pull out the cardamom pods.

2½ cups peeled, shredded carrot

2½ cups almond milk

5 crushed cardamom pods (or ¼ tsp ground cardamom)

¼–½ cup coconut sugar

2 Tbsp ghee

1 heaping Tbsp golden raisins

8 whole cashews

8 pistachios or 1 Tbsp slivered almonds

¼ cup almond meal (or leftover pulp from Almond Milk on page 113)

In a medium saucepan, warm the carrots and almond milk on medium-high heat. Turn the head down to medium-low and simmer, uncovered, for 15 minutes, stirring occasionally.

Add the cardamom, sugar, and ghee; stir and simmer until the liquid thickens and the mixture is almost dry. Add the raisins, nuts, and almond meal, setting aside 1 tsp of the nuts for garnish. Stir and cook 3–5 minutes more.

Serve warm in dessert bowls, garnished with a few slivered almonds.

cardamom tea cookies

MAKES 1 DOZEN

I like my biscuits to be substantial. It's rare that I will bake anything that doesn't stand in for a meal with a dollop of homemade yogurt. These almond-based biscuits are quite satisfying and feature cardamom, a spice revered for its sattvic nature. The taste is bright and offers a pick-me-up without leaving you overstimulated or taking your blood sugar for a ride, as white sugary, floury treats are sure to do.

1½ cups almond meal	¼ tsp salt	1 tsp pure vanilla extract
½ tsp ground cardamom	3 Tbsp coconut oil, melted	1 tsp rose water
¾ tsp baking powder	2 Tbsp maple syrup	

Preheat oven to 375 degrees. Line a baking sheet with parchment paper.

In a medium-size bowl, whisk together the almond meal, cardamom, baking powder, and salt. Drizzle the coconut oil over the top, and stir to combine. Add the maple syrup, vanilla, and rose water, stirring until the dough begins to clump together when you pinch it with your fingers.

Roll rounded tablespoons of the dough into 1-inch balls. Place on the parchment paper, 2 inches apart, and flatten with your fingertips so you have thin, round cookies. Continue until you use up all the dough.

Bake for 8–10 minutes, removing from the oven just before the edges begin to brown. Allow the biscuits to cool slightly on a wire rack before taking them off the baking sheet.

cantaloupe cooler

You won't believe how wonderful this cooler is in hot weather, when the appetite for a meal has wilted. Two ingredients—that's it. Drink this on an empty stomach, and don't have anything for at least an hour after to enjoy a clear, cooling effect. If it's appropriate weather for a cool drink, put the melon in the fridge for an hour before using, or blend two ice cubes into the drink.

1 perfectly ripe cantaloupe

¼ tsp ground cardamom

Halve the cantaloupe and scoop out the seeds. Scoop the flesh directly into a blender with a big spoon. Add the cardamom and whip on high for 1 minute. Pour into two tall glasses and enjoy.

Do Not Mix the Melon

— ◆ ◆ ◆ —

While in general, Ayurveda does not recommend mixing any raw fruits with food, melons get special notice for being best eaten alone. Cantaloupe, honeydew, and watermelon can be mixed together and will digest quickly, but when mixed with other foods, they will create a sour stomach, or gas and bloating in some cases. It's OK to mix from time to time, but as a habit, melon mixing can promote digestive imbalances.

dandi latte

Take a break, have a seat, and enjoy this foaming latte-style cup. Put that drying, acidic, stimulating coffee aside, and make way for the supportive, healing properties of dandelion root. You won't be disappointed. Promise me you won't work while you drink this. Promise.

---

2 cups water

1 tsp ground cardamom

2 tsp coconut sugar

¼ cup full-fat coconut milk

1 Tbsp dandelion coffee
    powder (such as
    Dandi-blend)

In a medium saucepan, bring the water, cardamom, coconut sugar, and coconut milk to a boil. Turn off the heat, but leave the pot on the burner.

Add the coffee powder and foam the drink by using an electric milk foamer, whizzing with a hand blender for 1 minute, or processing in a blender carafe. If using the last option, begin blending on low speed, so the heat does not blow the lid off the blender; after about 5 seconds, slowly increase to high speed for 1 minute.

Note: If you own a high-speed blender, you can put all the ingredients in the carafe and blend on high for 5 minutes, until steaming.

Quitting Coffee versus Reducing Coffee

— • ◆ • —

Several of my clients have replaced coffee with dandelion instant coffee. I have also observed how, after a period without coffee, clients notice how it makes them jittery when they start drinking it again. That jittery energy builds up, sometimes without us even noticing. For those with a resilient nervous system, it's fine to enjoy a little coffee, but for the rest of us, this daily habit can begin to overstimulate the mind and dry out or acidify our digestive organs. When it comes to calming the mind, reducing caffeine can change your life! Try to start with a goal of reducing coffee rather than jumping right into a cold-turkey scenario. Go down to one cup a day, then half a cup, and so on. And be sure to have your replacement roasty beverage, like the Dandi Latte, on hand.

fresh grape juice

SERVES 2

Classical Ayurveda texts tell us the red grape is "king among fruits" for its ability to cool, cleanse, and rejuvenate the body. Fresh juice is an easy way to use up a bunch of ripe, seedless grapes. I think you will find this an excellent summer treat.

2 cups red seedless grapes   2 tsp fresh lemon juice

½ cup cold water

Rinse the grapes well in cold water, or soak in a bowl of cold water for 5 minutes. Pick the grapes off the stem and load into a blender. Add the cold water and blend on high for 1 minute, until smooth.

Strain through a metal sieve, using the back of a large spoon to press the juice through. Add the lemon juice and serve.

Grapes of Old

— ◆ ◆ ◆ —

Ayurveda says that of all the fruits, grapes are best and are listed among the naturally nutritious foods that are good for everyone. Sweet and sour grape varieties have different indications due to the differing qualities of sweet and sour tastes. Green grapes are simply sweet and do not contain the health benefits of red grapes. Look for a deep purple skin to ensure the most healthful juice.

10

recipes *to* vitalize *and* motivate tamas

tamas

—— ⋄✦⋄ ——

For all the go, go, go in our days, there has to be some slow, slow, slow
to keep the balance. Tamas is that energy that likes to sit still and do
nothing. We all need just the right amount of rest and relaxation to
feel calm as well as vital, but too little activity can sit like a wet blanket.
If you are feeling lackluster, sad, cloudy, or stuck, turn to these recipes
to get your fires going again, to wake up and boost your brain power.
Stay motivated by eating these fresh, light meals that cook up quickly.
The recipes deliver a little kick from pickles, peppery soups, teas, and
fresh berries, and put a spring in your step with the vitality of sprouts,
citrus, and homemade green drinks.

motivating tamas

———— ◦ ✦ ◦ ————

Tamas feels like:
sluggish, lethargic, unmotivated,
sad, stagnant, bored

Potential Signs and Symptoms of Imbalance

- Brain fog, heavy feeling in head or chest
- Lack of energy
- Loss of appetite or cravings for fried or processed foods
- Lack of motivation or inspiration
- Sadness
- Helplessness
- Tendency to oversleep
- Inertia, feeling stuck, inability to make decisions
- Resistance to new ideas and change
- Procrastination

Tastes to Enjoy

Bitter, astringent, pungent

Foods to Favor

Leafy greens

Berries

Citrus fruits

Fresh herbs and spices

Turmeric

Seasonal vegetables, especially greens

Raw honey

Light grains, especially amaranth, quinoa, barley, rye,
   and wild rice

Vegetarian proteins like legumes and seeds

Foods to Reduce

Alcohol

Drugs

Processed cookies and candy

Protein bars

Pastries

Soft drinks

Processed snack foods, including chips

Old food and leftovers

Frozen food

Sweets

Cold dairy

Meat

General Lifestyle Guidelines

Exercise daily, especially first thing in the morning.

Eat regular meals, but not too much at once.

Eat light at night and preferably not after 7 P.M.

Eat only when you're hungry.

Moderate your use of TV and movies.

Get to bed early and rise early, with the sun.

Do not sleep in the daytime.

blueberry chia pudding

SERVES 1

Chia seeds do not appear in traditional Ayurveda recipes, but they have so many wonderful benefits. They offer the slick kind of fiber that helps the intestines usher out the
old, which certainly supports clarity of mind. In recent times, blueberries have been
noticed for their ability to improve memory. The addition of ginger here will warm
the pudding up to increase digestibility. The sky is the limit with the modifications
to this recipe. Strawberries and blackberries are both great in this satisfying breakfast;
sometimes I even substitute pomegranate juice for the milk.

2 Tbsp chia seeds	½ tsp pure vanilla extract	½ tsp grated fresh ginger
¾ cup almond milk	½ tsp Sweet Spice Mix	
¾ cup blueberries	1 tsp raw honey	

Soak the chia seeds in the almond milk while you gather the other ingredients, whipping
with a fork a few times to evenly distribute seeds.

Put the blueberries, vanilla, spice mix, and honey in the carafe of a blender (honey on
top so it doesn't stick to the blades). Add the chia mixture. Blend on high for 2 minutes.
The chia seeds should disappear, creating a smooth, whipped texture. If they don't, you
didn't soak the seeds long enough, so let the pudding sit for 5–10 minutes. To speed up
the process, you can warm the almond milk for soaking.

Travel Tip: If you don't have access to a blender, you can put all the ingredients in
a jar and shake thoroughly, then add it to your lunch bag with a spoon for a satisfying
dessert, or eat it as a to-go breakfast.

ghee pongal

SERVES 4–6

Pongal is a famous breakfast food from Tamil Nadu in southern India. Loved by all ages, it has simple spices and is easy on the gut. For those trying to ease off the sweet taste for morning meals, here is a savory, slightly peppery breakfast enjoyed by millions. A late January holiday marks the beginning of the warm season where rice pongal is served in two varieties, salty and sweet, and the cows are decorated with turmeric.

1 cup jasmine rice	1 Tbsp ghee	1 Tbsp cumin seeds
1 cup yellow split mung beans	2-inch piece fresh ginger, peeled and diced	12–15 curry leaves (if you can find them)
6 cups water	8–10 peppercorns	2 tsp pink salt

Rinse the rice and beans well, until the water runs clear. Soak them together in 2 cups of the water overnight, or for at least 1 hour.

In a medium heavy-bottomed saucepan, warm the ghee on medium heat. Add the ginger, peppercorns, cumin, and curry leaves, and sauté for just a few minutes, until you can smell them. Add the rice and beans with their soaking water, and the remaining 4 cups of water. Bring to a boil uncovered. Turn the heat down and simmer, covered, for 20 minutes, or until the mung beans are soft.

Stir in the salt. The pongal should have a soft, moist consistency. Serve in a wide bowl.

Jasmine versus Basmati Rice

— ◆◆◆ —

Jasmine rice works more like the local variety of rice used in southern India for pongal, because it has a shorter grain and cooks into a mushier, stickier dish. "Sticky" is not the quality we seek when cultivating clarity of mind, and this is why most recipes in this book call for the characteristically light and fine qualities of basmati rice or other whole grains. However, I want you to enjoy an authentic pongal experience. If you do choose to use basmati, cook it for an hour to get that softness.

overnight barley kanjee

SERVES 2

Barley is a dry grain that can help reduce congestion and brain fog. It can also help with the loss of appetite and energy that can result from the heavy, moist qualities of a damp season; stagnation from lack of exercise; or ama in the digestive tract. If your stomach is feeling heavy or your mind is foggy (and these two can go together), this recipe is a nice way to ease into a new day or reduce stress at the end of an old one. A regular morning kanjee in place of a complicated breakfast like granola will do amazing things for mind and gut fog. Kanjee also makes a great dinner. You might make a double batch and serve your second half later with Vitalizing Spice Mix and a side of steamed veggies, ghee, and lemon. There's no need to refrigerate any leftovers in most climates; just leave the pot on the stove until the evening meal.

½ cup barley	1 tsp Sweet Spice Mix or	**optional mix-ins**
6 cups water	Vitalizing Spice Mix	Small handful raisins
½ tsp salt	(optional)	Cinnamon stick
		Sprinkle of hemp seeds
		(sprinkle after cooking)

The evening before, rinse the barley and put it in a saucepan with 2 cups of the water. Bring to a boil for 5 minutes, cover, then turn off the heat and leave it there until morning.

When you get up, add the remaining 4 cups of water, salt, spice mix, and any optional mix-in you want. Simmer on medium-low heat, partially covered, for 2 hours or more. Add more hot water as needed to keep the barley covered. By the time you are ready for breakfast, it will be done. The longer you let it cook, the lighter its qualities. Add more water if necessary.

spiced stewed plums

We're talking about prunes here. Rebranded as "dried plums," the prune is a friend to many a sluggish gut. Before you do anything crazy to remedy a slow-moving bowel, try making a batch of this and having three warm, stewed prunes in warm grain for breakfast. Be careful, however, because mixing stewed prunes into a mélange of other foods can create uncomfortable gas. Keep it simple by omitting any milk or nuts from the meal. Keep things moving on the inside, and your outer life will also benefit with vitality and motivated energy.

1½ cups water	½ orange, thinly sliced, rind	1-inch piece fresh ginger,
1 cup dried plums (aka	and all	peeled and cut into
prunes)	3 cloves	matchsticks
Juice of ½ lemon		½ tsp ground cinnamon

In a medium saucepan, bring the water to a boil on high heat. Add all the other ingredients, and bring it back to a boil. Turn the heat down and simmer, covered, for 30 minutes, or until the plums and orange slices are soft. Take off the heat and let stand for 5 minutes or more before eating.

You can refrigerate it for 1 week.

Cold Prunes Don't Work

— ◆ ◆ ◆ —

In the case of constipation due to anxiety, worry, or stress, the gut contracts and takes on hard, dry qualities. Eating foods that are dry or cold will feed that imbalance rather than reduce it. Giving the gut nice warm, moist feelings will coax it back to motility. To enjoy some relief from prunes, make sure they are well moistened by soaking or cooking, and serve them warm.

refreshing sprout salad

SERVES 2

Enjoy this crunchy salad as a light meal for warm weather. Raw foods require a strong digestive fire and are best eaten alone, not mixed with cooked foods that digest at a different rate. The occasional raw salad can be refreshing, and thanks to root vegetables, sesame oil, and cashews, this recipe also has a grounding quality.

2 cups packed baby spinach	**dressing**
½ cup mixed mung and	1 Tbsp tamari
lentil sprouts	2 Tbsp sesame oil
½ cup shredded carrots	¼ cup lemon juice (about
½ cup shredded beets	1 lemon)
¼ cup cashew pieces	½ tsp Vitalizing Spice Mix

Create two beds of greens by dividing the spinach onto two plates. Top with a ¼ cup mound of sprouts, carrots, and beets in a colorful triangle.

Place the dressing ingredients together in a glass jar and shake to mix. Drizzle the dressing over the vegetables.

Roast the cashews in a small frying pan on medium heat until they begin to brown, about 5 minutes. Sprinkle the cashews over the salads, and serve immediately.

Oil Pulling for Strong Teeth

— ◆ ◆ ◆ —

Thousands of years ago, Charaka recorded that the practice of oil pulling, a swishing of oil in the mouth for as long as 20 minutes, ensures "the teeth do not ache or become sensitive and can chew the hardest food items." This suggests a protective action on tooth enamel, which hits home for me. When riding the overnight trains alone in India at age twenty, I began to grind my teeth while sleeping due to stress and worry. I didn't have the best teeth to begin with and had lost some enamel to braces, but sensitivity and enamel strength have called me to oil pulling. I definitely notice a difference. When crunching on something like this sprout salad, I give thanks for strong teeth! (See instructions on page 299.)

lemon parsley quinoa

Quinoa with dal or lentils (a variation on kichari) comes out amazingly creamy and satisfying. I've seen a lot of quinoa cooked a bit dry for a crunchy appeal. In Ayurveda, this is not recommended, as most grains should be cooked well and served moist for optimal digestion. I think you will find this bright and lemony one-dish meal super easy and kind of amazing. This is a great crowd pleaser!

1 cup quinoa	½ tsp cumin seeds	½–1 tsp salt
½ cup yellow split mung beans or red lentils	Zest of ½ lemon	Chopped fresh parsley, for garnish
4 cups water	¼ cup fresh lemon juice (about 1 lemon)	
1 Tbsp Vitalizing Spice Mix	1–2 Tbsp ghee	

Rinse the quinoa and beans in a fine mesh sieve. Set aside to soak for 1 hour or more.

In a large saucepan, boil the water on high heat. Add the quinoa, beans, spice mix, and cumin seeds to the boiling water. Keep on high heat until the liquid comes back to a boil. Immediately turn the heat down and simmer, partially covered, for 20 minutes without stirring. Check after 20 minutes to see if the dal is submerged. If not, pour a small amount of hot water on top, but do not stir. Simmer, covered, for 10 minutes more.

Remove from the heat. Add the lemon zest and juice, ghee, and salt; stir well with a fork, and let stand, covered, for a few minutes. This dish should have a slightly soupy, soft, and creamy consistency. Serve it in bowls as you would a stew. Garnish with chopped parsley.

roasted cherry tomato dal

SERVES 4–6

I noticed my tomato dal was a favorite recipe among readers of my first book, so I set about making a sattvic version for this book. In summer, I recommend using yellow and orange cherry tomatoes—they have less acid than the red ones, which makes them less heating and more sweet than sour. If you eat them often, tomatoes do increase rajas due to their sour taste, but the sweetness of a well-roasted tomato can be uplifting in moderation. This meal is a feast for the eyes, fun to make and eat, and a great way to use a bumper crop of cherry tomatoes.

2 cups yellow or orange
  cherry tomatoes
1 tsp + 1 Tbsp olive oil
1 tsp salt, divided into ¼ tsp
  and ¾ tsp
4 cups water

1 cup red lentils
1 tsp ground turmeric
1 cup green beans, trimmed
  and chopped into ½-inch
  pieces

⅓ cup packed fresh basil
  leaves, torn or roughly
  chopped
Freshly ground black pepper
  (optional)

Preheat oven to 400 degrees.

Toss the tomatoes with the 1 tsp of olive oil and ¼ tsp of salt. Spread in a single layer on a baking sheet. Roast until the tomatoes collapse, about 15–20 minutes.

In a large saucepan, bring the water to a boil over high heat. Rinse the lentils well and add to the water; boil, uncovered, for 5 minutes. Add the turmeric. Reduce the heat and simmer, covered, for 15 minutes. Add the green beans and simmer, covered, for another 20 minutes.

Remove from the heat and let stand for 5 minutes. Add the roasted tomatoes, stir in the 1 Tbsp of olive oil and ¾ tsp of salt. Divide the basil among the bowls as a garnish, and finish with freshly ground black pepper if desired.

Serve over white basmati rice or quinoa.

nourishing carrot and dal soup

SERVES 4

While I do love creamy carrot ginger soup, I rarely take the time to make it because I'm still hungry after I eat it. An all-carrot base is too light for me. This soup is my answer to the hunger challenge. The quick-cooking split mung beans add creamy texture as well as protein, and they are nourishing for all body types and all seasons.

1 cup split mung beans, soaked overnight or at least a few hours	4 peppercorns	½ tsp salt, plus more to taste
	1 Tbsp Vitalizing Spice Mix	Freshly ground black pepper, for garnish (optional)
	3 cups water	
1 Tbsp ghee	½ cup almond, hemp, or cow's milk	Fresh cilantro or parsley, for garnish (optional)
1 cup chopped carrot		

Drain and rinse the soaked mung beans.

Warm the ghee in a large saucepan. Sauté the carrots, peppercorns, and spice mix in the ghee until you can smell the spices, stirring to coat all pieces with ghee. Add the beans, and sauté for 1–2 minutes, stirring until coated. Add the water and simmer, partially covered, for 20 minutes. Add the milk and salt and simmer 5 minutes more. Remove from heat.

Using a hand blender, puree the soup until smooth. You can also do this in a blender carafe, but the mixture must cool a bit first. The milk should help it cool.

Pour into bowls and garnish with freshly cracked pepper and fresh cilantro or parsley, if desired.

Note: Ginger-carrot lovers can simply add 1 Tbsp grated ginger to the cook pot.

Skim the Foam

— ◆ ◆ ◆ —

Rinsing beans and grains well before cooking them will remove most residual impurities left after harvesting. However, some impurities will remain. In Hindu legend, a poison called *halahala* was created when demons and devas churned the ocean to obtain the nectar of immortality, *Amrita*. In the early cooking process, a foam gathers on top of the water when dal boils. It's a good idea to skim it off with a large mixing spoon and wash it down the sink. I like to think of my food as Amrita while I skim the foam to purify my dal.

sprouted lentil bowl
with pickled vegetables

SERVES 4

The satisfying qualities of this fiber-rich lentil and brown rice combo are vitalized by the use of sprouted lentils and colorful, pickled vegetables. Apple cider vinegar boosts digestive fire; reduces sweet cravings; and energizes the system with pungent, sour taste. Daikon radishes also improve digestion by mobilizing the breakdown of heavy, fatty foods. These pickled vegetables can be served alongside any grounding dish and are especially helpful for a rich meal.

lentil bowl	pickles	
4 cups water	2 medium carrots	2 Tbsp rice vinegar or apple cider vinegar
¾ cup brown rice	2 medium daikon radishes	¼ tsp salt (if using cider vinegar)
¾ cup Sprouted Lentils	(each about the size of a large carrot)	
1 Tbsp Vitalizing Spice Mix		
1 Tbsp ghee	1-inch piece fresh ginger,	
1 tsp cumin seeds	peeled and cut into	
1 tsp salt	matchsticks (optional)	

For the lentil bowl:

In a large saucepan, bring the water to a boil. Rinse the rice well, and add rice and lentils to the water. Bring to a boil again, uncovered. Add the spice mix. Reduce the heat to low and simmer, covered, for 45 minutes. Remove from the heat.

   Warm the ghee in a frying pan on medium heat. Sauté the cumin seeds until you can smell them, about 3 minutes. Add the ghee and salt to the rice, and fluff with a fork.

   Serve with 2 Tbsp of pickled vegetables.

For the pickled vegetables:

Peel the carrots and daikon radishes; cut into thin rounds or half-moons. Place them in a bowl, add the ginger, and sprinkle with the vinegar and salt (if using). Mix well and let stand for 10 minutes or more.

   These veggies keep in the fridge up to 1 week in a glass jar.

Daikon for Digestion!

— ◆ ◆ ◆ —

Daikon radishes are readily available in the produce section of most grocery stores, and they look like large, white carrots. If you eat sushi, you will often find crunchy ribbons of spiralized daikon on the side (*that's* what that stuff is). It's a spicy, incredibly low-calorie, high-detox food that can help the body reduce ama. Peel the skin and slice; add it to kicharis or dals, or even enjoy it raw, as in this pickle recipe.

RECIPES TO VITALIZE AND MOTIVATE TAMAS

beet coriander soup with sautéed greens

SERVES 2

There's nothing like digestive stagnation to promote that tamasic feeling, but beets and coriander keep things moving. I love to eat beets; they are great for digestive function and elimination. I don't, however, like the mess of preparing them. Behold as I introduce my no-more-pink-hand solution. This is my go-to beet plan: boil them whole, slide off the skins, and chop. The greens are also highly nutritious, so learn how to use them here. Join me, and feel the beet.

soup	3 cups almond milk	greens
4 cups water	½ tsp ground coriander	2 tsp coconut oil or ghee
1 bunch beets, with greens	½ tsp salt	Salt and freshly ground black pepper to taste

In a large saucepan, bring the water to a boil on high heat.

With kitchen shears, cut the green tops off the beets, right down to the flesh, and set aside for making fried beet greens. Wash the beets, and drop them into the water, untrimmed. Turn the heat down and simmer, covered, for 45–60 minutes, until soft. The time will depend on the size of your beets. Check softness with a fork or knife tip after 45 minutes.

Remove from the heat. Let the beets cool by submerging them in a bowl of cold water in your kitchen sink. When cool enough to touch, pour them in a colander to drain the water. Trim off the tops and tails. Under cold running water, slide the skins off the beets one by one. Cut the cooked beets into halves or quarters and place them in a blender.

Add the almond milk, coriander, and salt; blend to a smooth puree. Return to the saucepan and heat to the desired temperature. Serve with fried beet greens on the side.

For the fried greens:

Working with the green tops from your beets, cut off the thick stems (thicker than the width of your pinky) and discard, skinny ones can stay.

Wash the beet greens either by using a salad spinner or by submerging them in a large, shallow bowl of water. Shake them and allow sediment to fall to the bottom. Then rinse well in a colander, rubbing each leaf to check for soil. Chop the leaves and skinny stems into 2-inch pieces.

In a medium frying pan, warm the oil on medium heat. Add the greens, separating the pieces to coat evenly. Fry for 4–5 minutes, stirring occasionally, until tender. Remove from the heat and serve hot.

Beet greens have a sweet, earthy taste that may take a little getting used to. I have loved them from day one.

jeera (cumin) rice

3 CUPS

Turn ordinary rice into a beautiful, medicinal side dish. Cumin seed is prized as a spice to enkindle agni and is balancing for all body types. Cooking basmati rice with spices to motivate the appetite will also motivate the mind by ensuring you get the most nutrition out of your food, as well as by reducing tamas with pungent and bitter tastes. Not to mention it's a crowd pleaser, especially when served alongside Roasted Cherry Tomato Dal or High-Energy Dal.

1 tsp ghee	1 cup basmati rice, rinsed twice	4 peppercorns
2 tsp cumin seeds	1 cinnamon stick	2 cups water

Warm the ghee in a 2-quart pot on medium heat. Add the cumin seeds, and sauté for a minute or two, until you can smell them. Add the rice, cinnamon, and peppercorns, and sauté until the rice is coated. Add the water, turn the heat up to high, and bring to a boil. Reduce the heat and simmer, covered, for 20 minutes.

Remove from the heat. Fluff with fork, and pull out the cinnamon stick before serving.

Make Your Own Thali, the Ayurvedic Lunch

——— ◆◈◆ ———

The word *thali* comes from the word for the circular plate on which meals are served. A thali is usually served at midday and refers to a meal that contains all six tastes. A thali can change depending on the region of India in which it is served, varying in accompaniments and degree of spice. Most restaurants only serve thali at lunchtime. A restaurant thali will usually contain a folded chapati (whole-wheat flatbread); a *papad*, a crisp-fried, disk-shaped tortilla made of lentil flour; and a pile of basmati rice in the middle of the plate. This base is then surrounded by any number of small metal cups holding dal, cooked vegetable dishes, freshly made yogurt or buttermilk, perhaps a sweet such as rice pudding, and a spoonful of pickle right on the plate. Wait staff move around the restaurant with pots of each dish, filling the metal cups as eaters make room

for more by pouring them over the rice. I fend waiters off by holding my hands over the empty cups when I see them coming!

A sattvic thali is a bit tamer and focuses on the inclusion of the six tastes. At Ayurveda centers, lunch often comes on a stainless steel platter with a grain and a few cups containing diluted, spiced yogurt; a grain; a cooked vegetable or two, usually sautéed in ghee or coconut oil with mustard seed and curry leaf; and perhaps a thin, split mung dal. Having a few friends over and making an authentic thali together is an excellent way to enjoy sattvic cooking. Do the Lemon Pickle a day or so before. Make a batch of plain or cumin rice, any dal recipe, one or two vegetable recipes, and Lassi. When you don't have the little metal cups, place one cup of rice at the center of the plate and a half-cup of each other dish in a circle around it. Add a dollop of Lemon Pickle to the plate. Serve a small cup of Lassi on the side to be sipped at the end of the meal for improved digestion. Cara cooked the delicious thali you see here. I suggested combining the following recipes: Mixed Market Vegetables with Herbed Yogurt Sauce (page 224), Spiced Pumpkin Glee (page 184), Jeera (Cumin) Rice (page 276), Your Daily Dal (page 220), and Lemon Pickle (page 282).

beet hummus and pickles on rye

SERVES 6–8 AS AN APPETIZER, OR 3–4 AS A MEAL

White beans are versatile, creamy, and so satisfying. Large beans are naturally on the light, dry side, and paired with bright beets, tangy pickle, and plenty of lemon juice, they make a real pick-me-up. Colorful meals like this have the added benefit of invigorating the senses. Serve this colorful dish atop rye crackers or toasted rye bread with a leaf of lettuce or fresh garden herbs, as an open-faced sandwich.

1 medium beet, boiled and peeled	¼ cup tahini	1 tsp freshly ground black pepper
2 cups cooked cannellini beans	¼ cup olive oil	2 Tbsp Pickled Beets
	¼ cup fresh lemon juice	
	1 tsp rock salt	

Cut the boiled beet into quarters and place in a blender or food processor. Add all the other ingredients in the order listed. Process until smooth. If using a blender, begin by pulsing to break up the beans. When the mixture begins to blend, process on high until smooth. Add additional olive oil and lemon juice if the mixture is too thick to blend.

To wow your guests with an exotic-looking appetizer, serve in a broad bowl with Pickled Beets and a drizzle of olive oil in the center. Offer rye crackers and crisp romaine leaves on the side.

high-energy dal

Spicy, sweet, and buttery, this dal is destined to be a favorite. Green mung beans are known to promote strength and provide sustained energy. When a student is having difficulty mastering a strong pose, my yoga teacher recommends wheat chapatis (flatbreads) and green mung beans. This flavorful dal combines sweet potato with mung beans to build muscle tissue and deliver vegetarian satisfaction for strong appetites. The warming, stimulating qualities of garlic and onion will keep your energy moving in cold weather.

1 cup green mung beans,
    rinsed and soaked in
    water overnight
4 cups water
1 cup cubed sweet potato
1 Tbsp Vitalizing Spice Mix
1 tsp ground turmeric
1 tsp salt

tempering
2 Tbsp ghee
1 small garlic clove, finely
    chopped
¼ cup chopped onion
1 dry red chili
1 tsp black mustard seeds

1 tsp cumin seeds
1 tsp coriander seeds

In a large saucepan, bring the water to a boil on high heat. Drain and rinse the mung beans. Add the beans to the water and bring back to a boil. Cook, uncovered, for 5 minutes. Add the sweet potato, spice mix, and turmeric. Reduce the heat and simmer, uncovered, for 45 minutes or more. Add more hot water if needed to keep the beans and potato covered.

In a frying pan, warm the ghee on medium heat. Fry the garlic and onion until translucent, stirring occasionally. Add the chili and spices, and continue to fry until slightly brown, about 3 minutes more.

Take off the heat and add the tempering to the mung beans; stir to combine. Let stand for 5 minutes. Serve with basmati rice, or as a soup with a sprouted grain tortilla.

Note: Garlic and onions are not generally part of the sattvic diet because they excite the senses, agitate the mind, and stimulate libido. If you are feeling heavy, dull, or foggy, however, they can be just the thing to motivate that sluggish energy into activity. Favor them in cool weather, and use them therapeutically, not simply for their strong flavor.

cranberry orange raisin relish

MAKES 2 CUPS

Cranberries are cleansing. There is a bright and energizing quality to these little red friends that are harvested at summer's end after soaking up the fire element for a few months. This relish even *looks* exciting. Use it as a condiment to jazz up grains, vegetables, or tofu. Try it alongside sprout salad, on a buckwheat dosa, or in Overnight Barley Kanjee (page 262).

1 cup golden raisins

½ cup fresh orange juice

¼ cup apple cider vinegar

1 cup fresh (or frozen) cranberries

1 tsp grated orange zest

1 tsp ground ginger

¼ cup raw honey

In a medium saucepan, bring all the ingredients except the honey to a boil over medium heat, stirring frequently. Reduce the heat and simmer, uncovered, for 20 minutes. Remove from the heat, and let cool for 5 minutes. Stir in the honey until evenly distributed.

Store in the refrigerator in a glass, airtight container. This relish keeps for at least 1 week.

lemon pickle

MAKES ONE 8-OZ JAR

In a sattvic meal, redolent with sweet taste, we need just a little bit of the sharp and pungent qualities of this pickle recipe. It packs a real punch with whole lemons, chili, and ginger. Place one heaping teaspoon on the plate alongside vegetable, legume, and grain dishes, or atop a bowl of kichari. The pungency will act as a digestive aid. Just put a bit on the tip of your spoon as you gather up a bite, or stir it right in. You can eat the whole lemon—rind and all.

4 organic lemons	1-inch piece fresh ginger, peeled and chopped into matchsticks	¼ tsp ground turmeric
2 cups water		¼ cup evaporated cane sugar or coconut sugar
1 Tbsp fresh lemon juice		
	1½ tsp salt	1 tsp chili powder

In a large saucepan, bring the whole lemons and water to a boil on high heat. (The lemons will be only partially submerged in the water.) Turn down the heat and simmer, covered, for 30 minutes, or until skins are soft. Remove from the heat, drain the water, and let the lemons cool.

In a large mixing bowl, cut the lemons into quarters and then in half again, so each lemon is cut into eight pieces. Keeping the juices in the bowl, remove the seeds and woody core. Add the extra lemon juice and mix well. Add the ginger, salt, and turmeric, and mix well. Add the sugar slowly, a tablespoon at a time, mixing so all of the granules dissolve in the juice. Mix in the chili powder.

Refrigerate in a glass jar. Wait 1 full day before eating, and the pickle will keep for 1 month in the fridge.

Pickle Talk

— ◆ ◆ ◆ —

At most meals in India, especially in cool or rainy weather, you find a pickle on the plate—usually sour mango, lemon, or lime. With this six-taste condiment, a meal is completely balanced. More is not better though, as the digestive powers of salty and sour can cause imbalance if eaten in excess. Stick to a teaspoon and try it alongside any savory meal as a digestive, especially if your appetite is dull or your body or mind feels heavy.

chocolate mint
double-dipped strawberries

MAKES 6–8 STRAWBERRIES

Mint and strawberries are a classic combination of bright and cool, not to mention the colors! Use your summer harvest to make this light dessert; take 15 minutes more to double dip for optimal chocolatiness. This makes a fancy but light dessert or teatime treat when you have company.

1 batch Basic Coconut Chocolate	8 large organic strawberries, chilled	8 mint leaves

Line a dinner plate with parchment paper. Prepare the chocolate according to the instructions on page 143.

The trick to coating the strawberries is to keep the Coconut Chocolate in a liquid state. As the coconut oil begins to cool, it will harden the mixture. Keep a pan of hot water on the stove, and warm the base of the bowl of chocolate in the hot water if it begins to cool and get sticky.

Hold the leaf of each strawberry and suspend it over the bowl of chocolate. Use a large spoon to drizzle the chocolate over and around the strawberry to evenly coat; let the excess drip back into the bowl. Keep the top stem and leaves uncovered as you hold it.

Lay each strawberry on its side on the parchment-lined plate. Press a mint leaf onto the center of each berry. Refrigerate for 15 minutes until the chocolate is hard.

Drizzle the chilled strawberry with the chocolate again, being careful not to break the leaf. You may need to rewarm the chocolate. Leave a little tip of the mint leaf showing for color appeal. Put the strawberries back on the plate and refrigerate for another 15 minutes, or until ready to eat.

Remove from the fridge, and let stand for 5 minutes before eating.

honey almond bites

Honey is cleansing and is considered in Ayurveda to be a most beneficial food. It creates warming, gunk-scraping actions in the body and can be used to cleanse cholesterol and mucous. Honey's penetrating quality makes it a digestive aid rather than heavy and dense like other sweets, which can overload the system and promote tamas. Go easy on this one, and make it to order to avoid overeating.

½ cup rolled oats	¼ cup raw almond butter
¼ cup raw honey	½ tsp Sweet Spice Mix

Set aside ¼ cup of the oats. Put the rest of the oats and the remaining ingredients in a mixing bowl, and mash together with a fork or spatula until thoroughly blended. (It takes a little elbow grease.) Refrigerate the batter for 15–20 minutes.

Form balls by rolling 2 tsp of chilled batter between your hands. Place the ¼ cup of oats in a shallow bowl, and roll the balls in the oats to coat.

Keep the balls in the fridge or eat immediately. Serve with a cup of hot herbal tea.

Enjoy These All-the-Time Foods

— ◆ —

I know you are wondering what that short list of most beneficial foods is. According to classical texts, the following foods can be consumed often for optimal health: rice, wheat, barley, *amalaki*, sugar, ghee, milk, honey, and salt. Keep in mind that all of these foods, especially wheat, sugar, and milk, were considered beneficial in their natural, unadulterated forms a few thousand years ago. Today, these foods remain excellent but require good sourcing and minimal processing (see chapter 4 for more information). Amalaki, also known as Indian gooseberry, is an olive-size green fruit that is very sour and high in vitamin C. Amla is most often consumed in the traditional rejuvenative jam, *chyawanprash*, which is available through Ayurvedic suppliers.

drinking cacao

If the chocolate bug has got you, this is a sattvic way to have a chocolate treat. Far preferable to store-bought processed chocolate, in this version, the pure fats of cacao and coconut will break down and be absorbed into your tissues. The right kind of fats, digested well, increase mental focus. We all know it tastes good, but this particular cup will make you feel good too.

1 Tbsp cacao powder	1 cup hot water
1 Tbsp coconut sugar	2 tsp coconut oil

Measure the cacao and sugar into a bowl or glass measuring cup. Pour in ¼ cup of the hot water, and stir or whisk until a thick paste forms. Pour in the remaining hot water, and whisk in the coconut oil. Alternatively, you may blend the oil into the beverage with an immersion blender or electric milk frother for a smoother drink.

Pour the cacao into a mug, and enjoy.

Sip Hot Water for Health

— ◆ ◆ ◆ —

Cold quality hardens the body, dries the mucous membranes, and slows the digestion. The simple therapy of sipping hot water can rehydrate and revitalize. Tamas is like water turning to ice; free-moving energy begins to slow down, solidify, and stagnate. This process leaves you feeling dull, uninspired, stuck. It can happen due to mental factors, such as grief, or physical factors, such as ama. Try keeping a thermos of hot water nearby for a few days and sip continuously to melt ama and encourage good circulation.

no-donut holes

That's right, no dough. *Dough* rhymes with *slow*. Dough is sticky and heavy, and it makes the mind and body feel slow. Sticky quality is hard to digest and makes for stagnation, procrastination, and eventually, sadness. How about a sweet treat that nourishes you with whole foods and fiber? If that doesn't motivate you to try No-Donut Holes, I don't know what will.

2 Tbsp coconut oil	½ cup almond meal	2 Tbsp finely shredded
2 Tbsp raw almond butter	¼ tsp salt	coconut
¼ cup maple syrup	1½ cups Oat Flour	
1 tsp pure vanilla extract	1 Tbsp cacao nibs	

In a large mixing bowl, combine the oil, almond butter, maple syrup, and vanilla. Add the almond meal, Oat Flour, and salt. Mix well with a fork until combined. Smooth the dough along the sides of the bowl with the fork to break up any chunks. Keep going until everything is evenly combined. Fold in the cacao nibs. Put the bowl in the freezer for 5 minutes to firm up.

Put the shredded coconut in a wide bowl. Roll a heaping tablespoon of the dough into a ball, continuing until you've used up all the dough. Roll each ball in the coconut to coat, lining them up on a plate or in a storage container as you go. Do not stack the balls.

Store in the refrigerator for up to 1 week. Allow No-Donut Holes to come to room temperature before enjoying.

Although there's something fun and exciting about eating No-Donut Holes, I'm not always in the mood to stand there and roll balls. I just press the mixture into a square container, sprinkle the coconut on top, refrigerate for an hour, then cut it into squares.

Doughn't Do It!

— ◆ ◆ ◆ —

Pastries are an instigator of tamas in the mind. The combination of processed white flour, white sugar, and butter or questionable oils makes a trifecta of heavy, indigestible qualities that gunk up the gut. For most, a daily habit of eating pastries is a ticket to slow, dull qualities.

vitalitea

Need a lift? Need to clear your head? Stuffed up? Overindulged? Try this invigorating combination of slightly and spicy savory to get yourself and your gut in gear. Good for any time of day, but know that this tea will stimulate the appetite on an empty stomach, so be ready.

2½ cups water	½ tsp cumin seeds	2–3 peppercorns
1-inch piece fresh ginger, washed	3 cloves	¼ tsp ground turmeric

In a small saucepan, bring the water to a boil on high heat. Coarsely chop the ginger, leaving the skin on. Add all the spices to the water. Reduce the heat, and simmer for 20–25 minutes. Strain into two mugs.

pine-delion green drink

Pineapple has sweet, sattvic qualities, as most fruits do. If it is unripe, however, it takes on a sour effect, which can disturb the stomach and, in excess, lead to the excitability and irritability of rajas. Dandelion greens have a bitterness not often found in the standard diet and bring light, clear qualities to the mind and body. Here, sweet and bitter dance together in a nice balance. Get the dandelion greens from an organic supplier while they are fresh, small, and tender. Large greens will yield a bitter shake.

2 cups water or coconut
water

1 cup diced ripe pineapple

1 cup packed dandelion
greens

Place all the ingredients in a blender in the order listed. Blend on high for 1 minute, until a fluffy, smooth puree results.

Serve immediately.

spicy turmeric lemonade

SERVES 4

The last thing you want to do when you feel lethargic is drink alcohol. Alcohol, excepting the occasional few ounces of medicinal wine or spirit, dulls the mind by overwhelming the body with simple sugars. Having other beverages to choose from, especially when entertaining, is very helpful in sustaining a new habit. On a warm day, sit with a friend, relax, and have a glass of this bright orange, spicy lemonade. It's quite a conversation starter. Allow time for cooling the spicy syrup as you plan for guests. And easy on the ice.

2-inch piece fresh ginger, crushed	3 cups water	½ cup fresh lemon juice (about 4 lemons)
½ tsp ground turmeric	¼ cup raw honey	1 cup ice

To make the syrup, boil the ginger and turmeric with 1 cup of the water, covered, in a small saucepan for 10 minutes. (Boil longer if you want it stronger.) Take off the heat, and cool for 3–5 minutes. Stir in the honey until dissolved. Refrigerate until cold.

Combine the ginger-turmeric syrup, fresh lemon juice, and the remaining 2 cups of water. Divide among four glasses, each with a few cubes of ice.

APPENDIX 1
DINACHARYA (DAILY ROUTINES)

The following dinacharya, or daily practices, appear here in their optimal order. You do not have to practice them all. Generally, tongue scraping and oiling of the skin are most important for everyday practice. For rajas imbalances, a weekly head massage is highly beneficial, and for tamas imbalances, dry brushing a few times weekly keeps the energy moving.

Materials

- *Tongue scraper:* A U-shaped, bevel-edged piece of copper or stainless steel used for cleaning the tongue.
- *Dry brush:* A stiff, natural bristle brush with a wooden handle, used for exfoliating the skin.
- *Massage oil:* Be sure to buy organic, high-quality oil that is less than one year old. Keep oil out of the sun. Buy refined sesame oil for oil pulling. (Visit the "Resources" section for trusted mail-order sources.)
- *Neti pot:* Drugstores sell nasal irrigation kits with plastic pots and packets of salt (both handy for travel), but it's best to purchase a ceramic or stainless steel pot for home use. You can find them at most health food stores or from a supplier in the "Resources" section of this book.
- *Glass dropper bottles:* Sterile, empty glass dropper bottles can be purchased at some health food stores and herbal suppliers. Use them to store sesame oil for the nose or rose water for the eyes.
- *Rose hydrosol:* A decoction made from the water of steamed rose petals, it is safe for use in the eyes and to flavor food. Hydrosol is different from rose water, which is made by adding rose essential oil to water and is unsafe for the eyes.

Tongue Scraping

Use a stainless steel or copper tongue scraper. First thing in the morning, before consuming any liquids, scrape your tongue five to six times, from as far back as you can reach to the tip. Scrape the entire surface of your tongue, especially way in the back. Press gently, but do not disturb the tongue tissue. Mucus will likely appear on the scraper; rinse in the sink as needed.

After finishing, clean the scraper thoroughly with hot water, and keep it near your toothbrush. Follow with tooth brushing and a cup of hot water or Vitalitea (page 291) or Yogi Tea (page 199). Do not scrape your tongue at other times of the day.

MASSAGE OIL

NETI POT

GLASS
DROPPER

NASYA
OIL

DRY BRUSH

TONGUE
SCRAPER

Eye Washing

Run cool water from the tap, and rinse your eyes well by splashing the cool water over open eyes with your hands four or five times. Follow by blinking seven times and rolling your eyes in circles. If you have burning, itching, or redness of the eyes, you can spray or drop rose water into them at this time. Be sure to purchase a hydrosol rather than water with rose essential oil added to it. Essential oils are not safe for the eyes.

Neti (Nasal Irrigation)

Think of *neti*, or irrigation of the nasal passages, as flossing for your nose. Using a neti pot involves pouring a small amount of salt water from a ceramic or stainless steel pot through each nostril, dislodging any accumulated mucus and impurities. I like to practice neti in the shower, where the warmth of the shower opens the nasal passages and any drips will be washed away.

Potential bugs can't get a hold on you when you use the neti pot. Practice neti in the morning, when the seasons change, when the cold and flu season begins, and as needed through the spring and fall. Mucus-prone or allergic types will find they benefit from daily use of the neti pot, while dry types will need this only occasionally and will benefit more from *nasya* (see the next section). This practice can also be used for a few days when your immunity feels compromised. Not everyone needs it every day. If you feel the water does not drain fully from your nasal passages, refrain from doing it.

To practice, boil purified water and add enough cold purified water to be sure the temperature is not too hot. You should be able to hold your finger in it comfortably. Be sure to check. Dissolve fine-grain, pure sea salt completely in the warm water (neti pots come in different sizes, so read the instructions on yours to find the correct amount of salt). In the shower or at the sink, lean forward, keeping the back of your neck extended, so your whole torso is bending. Tip your head to the side, place the spout in your top nostril and gently tip the neti pot to slowly pour the water in; wait for the water to run out the other nostril.

If the water is not draining easily after a few tries, refrain from practicing until you can get formal guidance. Let the water run out naturally. Do not forcibly blow your nose, as this can send the water in farther. You may cover one nostril and simply exhale to help the last bit of water out. Tip your head the other way, and repeat for the other nostril.

Note: Too much salt burns, whereas too little leaves you feeling like you have swimmer's ear. Do not practice neti more than once a day.

Nasya (Oiling of the Nose)

Administration of medicines through the nasal cavity can access the brain directly and is traditionally used for mental as well as physical imbalances. A general practice of oiling the nose balances the effects of dry, cold air and can induce a state of calm. For medical applications, an Ayurvedic practitioner trained in nasya therapies is required.

Unless you experience congestion, always follow neti with nasya, applying sesame oil to your nostrils by swirling it in with a Q-tip or pinkie fingertip and inhaling deeply. This will balance the drying effect of the salt from neti. Order oil from a supplier in the "Resources" section, or make your own nasya oil by decanting refined sesame oil into a sterile dropper bottle. Drop the oil onto your pinkie, a Q-tip, or directly into your nostril; do not touch the dropper. Keep the dropper next to your bed if you experience dry nasal passages at night. Even if you don't practice neti, take care to oil your nose while doing daily oil massage. Don't forget to take your nasya oil on plane rides and use it before riding on public transportation. The oil is generally good for one year.

Nasya is not indicated in cases of chronic congestion; it is better to see an Ayurvedic practitioner to help you discover the cause.

Gandush (Oil Pulling)

The swishing or holding of oil in the mouth for 5 to 20 minutes is used to balance the effects of excessive air and space elements in the region of the head and to detoxify the digestive system. As the minutes go by, the oil pulls saliva into the mouth, which cleanses the mouth of bacteria that can be responsible for tooth decay and bad breath. When held for a longer time, detoxification of the sinus can also result in a small amount of drainage. The amount of liquid in the mouth will increase as the saliva arrives, and the oil should be white when you spit it out. As a preventive measure for oral hygiene and tooth health, practice *gandush* daily. Even if you don't do it every day, it still benefits you.

Sesame oil's antibacterial properties are greater than those of coconut oil; however, coconut has a more appealing taste to some and can be used if necessary for palatability. Flavored blends for oil pulling are becoming available from Ayurvedic suppliers. As with any oral hygiene, morning is the ideal time to cleanse the mouth. To practice, begin by taking note of the time. Slug about 1 Tbsp of oil into your mouth, trying not to get the oil on your lips (just because the oily feeling can be unpleasant). Hold it there for a minute or so, then begin gently swishing it over your gums and between your teeth. Do not swallow while the oil is in your mouth. Be gentle so you do not exhaust your jaw or facial muscles—remember you are working toward 20 minutes. Do not engage in any activities that might result in tripping, falling, or accidentally

DINACHARYA (DAILY ROUTINES)

299

swallowing. I like to swish as I get ready to leave for work in the morning or while I'm washing some dishes. Twenty minutes ensures optimal benefits, but you may have to work up to this. See how long you make it in the beginning, but hold the oil for a minimum of 5 minutes. Spit the oil into the trash, not the drain, as it will eventually clog the pipes. Gargle with warm water and brush your teeth. Do not drink or eat anything without gargling and brushing first. If you have excessive or chronic tension of the jaw or facial muscles, do not swish; simply hold the oil in your mouth for the desired time.

Shiro Abhyanga (Head Massage)

This technique is excellent for relaxation and stress relief. Ayurvedic body treatments for the mind generally focus on the head, mouth, ears, and nasal passages for their proximity to the brain and the activity of the sense organs. *Shiro abhyanga* and oiling of the ears and nose can be used to calm the mind. Because oiling the scalp requires a good shampooing afterward, practice the head massage one or two times weekly, when it is convenient for you to wash your hair, such as a weekend morning. When sleep is a problem, head massage can be an excellent way to calm the mind at bedtime. To avoid going to bed with a wet head, you can wrap it in an old towel, scarf, or hat and wash the oil out in the morning. Take care not to let your head get cold in the night. Head massage with oil is contraindicated in cases of congestion, illness, brain fog, or lethargy.

Melt 2 Tbsp of coconut oil in a small vessel or ramekin. If you run cold, sesame oil is a good choice. Warm the oil slightly if it is cold out. Remove any hair ties and brush the tangles out of your hair. Begin by gently kneading your shoulders and neck with circular motions a few times. Dip your fingers into the oil and distribute it evenly over your fingertips. Spread your fingers and work your hands into your hair on either side of your head, above your ears, with your fingers pointing up. With a shampoo-like action, work your fingertips to the crown of your head. "Shampoo" the scalp around the crown gently with your oiled fingertips until you have covered the top of your head. This is the most important part of the scalp. Dip your fingers into the oil again, and "shampoo" the rest of your scalp until finished; this should take 5 minutes or more. Rub a bit of the oil onto the entirety of each ear with small, circular motions, and slide your pinkie tips into the ear holes to coat them with oil. Wrap your head if it's bedtime, or relax for 10 to 30 minutes with the oil on your head.

To clean your hair, first apply shampoo to your scalp and roots and work into the oily parts of your hair, without water. Add a small amount of water to make suds and shampoo. Add more water as needed to get enough suds for your whole head. Those with thick hair may need to shampoo again to remove the oil. Sesame oil may require a bit more shampooing than coconut oil.

Dry Brushing

This procedure is especially indicated in cases of tamas, including lethargy, weight gain, or water retention. Use a natural bristle dry brush (available in drugstores and health food stores) on dry skin. Beginning at your ankles and moving up toward your heart, make small, brisk circles to exfoliate and stimulate the skin of your entire body, especially your armpits and chest, inner thighs and groins, and anywhere stubborn fat tissue likes to hang around. Take 3 to 5 minutes and be firm, but do not disturb the skin. A rosy color should result. Practice anywhere from daily to once a week, before having your oil massage and shower.

Abhyanga (Oiling of the Skin)

If you do only one dinacharya practice, do this one. You will notice that oiling your skin creates a protective, strengthening force field around you for the day.

It's best to apply warm oil thickly right before you shower or in the shower. The warm water will open your pores, and the massage will penetrate more deeply. Warm the oil by sitting a small container of it in a sink of hot water while you get undressed. Apply the oil for 5 minutes before you shower, using long strokes along bones and circular strokes on joints. To avoid slipping, do not oil the feet. In cold weather, you may choose to keep a small plastic container of massage oil in your shower. When you're ready to perform your abhyanga, put the container on the shower floor and turn on the water, so you and the oil warm up together in the shower for a minute. Turn off the water; apply a palmful of oil to your entire body, including your ears and nostrils—but you may skip the rest of your face. Rub it in well for a few minutes, then turn on the warm water again, stand under it, and rub some more. Do not soap off your skin—just soap the hairy parts to remove the oil. Towel dry—lingering in your towel for a few minutes to let your skin absorb the oil, if necessary—get dressed, and go about your day.

WHAT KIND OF OIL TO USE

You may enjoy changing your massage oil with the seasons, as indicated in the seasonal lifestyle guides, but here are a few general choices. Please remember to do a patch test with any oil before applying it to your entire body to be sure you are not allergic.

Sesame oil: Traditionally sesame oil is favored for its ability to build strength and softness in the body. Sesame oil is warming and indicated for those who run cold and experience dry skin.

Sunflower and almond oil: These two lighter oils are neither heating nor cooling and are indicated for those who do not experience very dry skin.

Coconut oil: Coconut oil is cooling and indicated for those who run hot or have sensitive skin.

SNEHANA (SPECIAL ABHYANGA DURING A CLEANSE)

The following practice is recommended for daily use throughout a seasonal cleanse to quiet the nerves and to soften impurities and the channels that carry them out of the body, so they can be released.

Sneha means "love" in Sanskrit, and this ancient practice is literally an application of love. Taking the time for this kind of massage once a week throughout the year will greatly enhance the immune system, strengthen the nervous system, and help with pain management.

Warm ¼ to ½ cup of organic sesame oil in a jar or bottle placed in hot water. Make sure the room you oil in is cozy and warm. Prepare the room and remove your clothes before you begin to minimize the need to move (and the possibility of slicking surfaces with oil). Lay an old bath towel on the floor and sit down. Breathe deeply a few times and give thanks for the time and space to care for yourself in this way. Apply the warm oil to your body with love and patience. Rub it in well, especially in areas that trouble you. Beginning with your feet, work your way up your body, using long strokes along bones, circular strokes on joints, and wide, clockwise circles on your chest and abdomen. Massage your face and head last, rubbing the oil into your scalp. Use your little fingers to put oil in your ears and nose. Half a cup will seem like a lot. Keep going until you don't think your skin can absorb anymore; this process may take 15 minutes. When you've massaged in all the oil, lie back on your towel and relax for 5 to 30 minutes. It takes at least 20 minutes for the body to absorb the oil, so after 15 minutes of massage, relax for at least 5 minutes. Burn a candle or play soft music.

Now enjoy a hot shower, but wipe your feet first so you don't slip. Do not use soap; the hot water will remove any excess oil. Apply shampoo to your hair before wetting it to cut the oil. After you shower, pat yourself dry. Your skin may still seem a bit oily; massage the oil in further, and it will gradually be absorbed. Afterward, clean your bathtub or shower stall of residual oil to make sure no one slips!

Note: When your towel becomes very oily, it can create a fire hazard if you put it in the dryer after washing. Better to hang your abhyanga towels to dry and replace them periodically instead.

APPENDIX 2
MIND-CLEANSE: A THREE-DAY REBOOT PROGRAM

To optimize mental digestion, you need to create a little space. Think of trying to ignite a wood stove when it is overstuffed with sticks and crumpled newspaper—it just fizzles out. This is how the energy of the mind and body can feel when there is a backlog of materials needing to be digested, and the fires necessary to metabolize that backlog are low. The idea behind a mind-cleanse is to simplify. Simplify the diet and rest the mind along a simple daily rhythm that leaves a little space for quiet self-care. Simply follow the rhythm and whatever arises, relax, and breathe easy; you are cultivating sattva, the energy of contentment. Give yourself a pat on the back for any amount of heartfelt effort. Come out the other side with nicely stoked mental fires burning bright. Or at least get the pilot light on.

Preparing

It isn't necessary to implement all of the suggestions for this cleanse, and there's certainly no need to be perfect. In fact, the desire for perfection can be the driving force behind mental imbalance, leading to anxiety and/or exhaustion. Better to sit down, look over the general guidelines, and decide just what feels like enough to commit to right now. Perhaps you start with one day and work your way up to three next time. Maybe you surprise yourself and follow the guidelines for 5 days or create a new habit that sticks around. Once you find a comfortable commitment, write down your plan for a mind-cleanse based on the guidelines that follow.

Consider the menu and daily routines, and shop for what you need beforehand. Purchase all the materials needed for meals and dinacharya, such as massage oil and a dry brush.

Finding the Time

It is ideal to begin your cleanse when you have a day off, perhaps a weekend without social engagements (this will likely require planning ahead to set aside the time). Traditionally, cleanses are undertaken at the junctures of fall and spring. This is a time when both the external and internal worlds are ripe for change. Change out the boots and flip-flops, as well as the seasonal pantry, and focus on changing up your internal world as well. Post-holidays, around the New Year, is also a great time, as many are welcoming new resolutions. Consider inviting a friend to join you.

Mind-Cleanse Dietary Guidelines

Keeping the diet easy to digest will allow your body a chance to establish a sense of balance. In case something in your diet was causing poor digestion, such as dairy's heavy qualities producing brain fog or coffee leading to restlessness, the simple diet will illuminate these dietary patterns and how they affect the mind.

Take a step back from substances that could be responsible for imbalance when consumed too often:

- Caffeine
- White sugar (does not include date sugar, raw honey, maple syrup, coconut sugar, agave, and so on)
- Alcohol
- Meat, wheat, and dairy

Eating Mostly Kichari

Those who have followed an Ayurvedic cleanse before, those who don't need lots of variety, and those who don't want to worry too much about what to cook will do well to eat the Ayurvedic superfood kichari for breakfast, lunch, and dinner. I recommend preparing a batch of kichari in the morning and eating a bowl at every meal, along with any of my seasonal vegetable sides, such as Creamy Tahini Kale, Spiced Pumpkin Glee, or Cumin Roasted Vegetables.

More adventurous and experienced cooks can choose from any of the recipes in this book if kichari doesn't cut it. Beware of getting too fancy with your meals—too many dishes or too gourmet, and you might end up tired of cooking. Keep it simple to ensure success. Enter kichari or any stew, the one-pot meal! You will find Kichari Four Ways in the sattvic recipes and can vary your breakfast with Apple Raisin Breakfast Kichari or Date Pear Morning Kichari. You can expect cravings for other foods, but do your best to stick to the program to allow your digestive system to relax.

For those who like variety, here are a few sample menus.

Sample Menu for Lighter Warm Weather Fare
Breakfast: Sattvic Smoothie
Lunch: Your Daily Dal and Quick Buckwheat Dosa with Mint Chutney
Dinner: Toasted Coconut and Cumin Pea Soup and Cardamom Tea Cookies

Sample Menu for Comforting Cool Weather Fare

Breakfast: Baked Buckwheat with Cardamom and Blueberries

Lunch: Hearty French Lentil Kichari with Pickled Beets

Dinner: Mung Bean Fritter and Gingered Sweet Potato Dal

DAILY MIND-CLEANSE GUIDELINES

(See appendix 1 for complete instructions for dinacharya practices.)

Morning Routines

- Scrape your tongue upon waking and follow this by sipping a cup of hot water, with lemon if you like. It is important to clean the mouth when attempting to clear the head.
- Do not turn on any devices first thing during the mind-cleanse. Before ingesting any information, practice Daily Gratitude for 5 minutes (see sidebar).
- Take a walk or do some exercise before ingesting any information.
- Do not eat breakfast until you are hungry.

Afternoon Routines

- Try not to snack between meals. Eat enough at mealtimes. This may take a little practice.
- Sit down while eating. Do not eat anything while standing during the mind-cleanse.
- Eat a big lunch and a smaller dinner.
- Enforce a 15-minute no-work break between 2 and 6 P.M. Step outside, close your eyes and lean back or lie down, or play with your pets. No media devices during this break.

Evening Routines

- About 2 hours after dinner, or before bedtime, give yourself a 30-minute oil massage (see appendix 1).
- No screens after 9 P.M. (this may be the hardest *and most important* part of allowing the mind to rest and digest). If you follow only one guideline, make it this one.
- Rinse and soak your grains and legumes for tomorrow's kichari to reduce cook time and increase digestibility. (See appendix 3 for more information on soaking.)

Avoid

- Eating while standing up, walking, or driving
- Eating too much at one time
- Skipping meals
- Overexerting and overscheduling yourself
- Watching TV and social media

Enjoy

- Sattvic activities such as outdoor time, reading, and arts and crafts
- Consistent, sit-down mealtimes
- Quiet time

Signs of a Successful Mind-Cleanse

Absence of brain fog, increased productivity

Sound sleep, feeling of being refreshed on waking

Calm and comfortable feelings, steady emotional state, less reactivity

Clear eyes

More attention to loved ones and nature

Less procrastination

Sustained energy

Desire for sattvic activities

How to Practice Daily Gratitude

◆ ◆ ◆

Upon waking, take a pen and paper, and find a quiet place where you can sit comfortably—in a chair or on a cushion on the floor—and are confident you won't be disturbed for a few minutes. Write down three things you are grateful for today. (It can be the same or different things every day.) Set an alarm for 5 minutes. Place your right hand over your heart and your left hand over your belly. Relax your chest and belly. Count three breaths. Bring your attention to the three things you are grateful for. As you let your mind rest on these parts of your life, bring your attention to your heart center. Notice the *feeling* of gratitude there. If you don't feel anything, just wait and concentrate on what makes you grateful. With practice, the feeling will begin to arise. Allow the feeling to spread from your heart into your belly. Sit in gratitude until the alarm sounds.

APPENDIX 3
TOOLS AND TECHNIQUES

CARAFE BLENDER: A blender with a glass carafe has more power than a hand blender and is called for in recipes in which the ingredients are too hard or fibrous for a hand blender, such as juices and chutneys.

CHEESECLOTH: Use several layers to strain nut and rice pulp when making milks, especially if you are using a high-speed blender.

FOOD PROCESSOR: This tool takes up a lot of space, but it has the most power for grinding nuts and makes chunkier chutneys and smoother, thicker pâtés and hummus than a carafe blender.

HAND BLENDER: Also known as an immersion blender or stick blender. Used to blend nut milks and puree soups, a hand blender is quicker to clean than a carafe blender. It works especially well for hot soups, which can make a carafe too hot.

PRESSURE COOKER: A staple in an Indian kitchen, a pressure cooker cuts cooking time in half for legumes and hard vegetables; does not require soaking; and ensures a well-cooked, easily digested bean.

RICE COOKER: An electric rice cooker can be preset to make rice or kichari by a certain time. This tool is a great time-saver.

Graters and Grinders

GRATER: Metal box graters are common, but a plane grater takes up less space in the kitchen. A good grater should have small and large grating options and be sturdy. Microplane graters work great for grating fresh ginger.

MORTAR AND PESTLE: Stone grinding is traditional in much of India's cooking, and it is still common to see home cooks sitting outside, grinding the day's ingredients. Every-day Ayurveda recommends that you enjoy the aromatic task of freshly grinding spices for your meals. A stone mortar and pestle will not retain scents like a wooden one does.

SPICE GRINDER: A coffee grinder reserved for spices, seeds, and nuts allows you to make large amounts of spice mixes quickly for storage.

PEPPER MILL: Freshly ground pepper at the table is a joy of life. Look for a wooden pepper mill and fill it with high-quality black or multicolor peppercorns.

Pots, Pans, and More

BAKING SHEET: You'll use this for cookies; look for high-grade stainless steel, not aluminum. Some recipes call for lining the baking sheet with parchment paper.

CAST-IRON FRYING PAN: Cast-iron pans are favorable cooking tools for slow cooking, frying, and baking because of their resiliency and ability to distribute heat evenly. A well-seasoned pan will have a nonstick quality. My recipes call for a large size, which can be anywhere from 15 to 17 inches in diameter. A smaller diameter can be used, though you may need to increase cooking times.

FINE MESH SIEVE: A colander's holes are too big for some grains and legumes, so a metal sieve or strainer is essential for rinsing these foods as well as vegetables. A metal sieve may also be used to strain the pulp from nut milks and separate dairy solids from ghee.

FRYING PAN: A frying pan is broad and wide, with a short lip, and is used for steam sautéing and frying. "Green" frying pans with a ceramic nonstick covering are preferable to other nonstick surfaces. Get rid of your Teflon, which can create harmful chemical compounds if the coating breaks down into your food.

GLASS BAKING DISH: My recipes call for an 8-inch square dish, as well as a 9-inch pie dish. One dish can substitute for the other in the recipes.

MUFFIN CUPS: Some of my muffin batters are too dense to bake in an unlined muffin tin and require the use of paper cups, which can be found in the baking aisle of the grocery store.

MUFFIN TINS: These are generally available with six or twelve cups; most of my recipes make six muffins. Look for stainless steel tins, not aluminum.

PARCHMENT PAPER: Parchment paper is used for lining a cookie sheet to keep foods from sticking; it is preferable to wax paper for baking.

SAUCEPAN: This is a soup pot with high walls, usually in 2-, 4-, and 6-quart sizes. A 4-quart pot is best for recipes that serve four or more, while a 2-quart pan can be used to make smaller amounts. Favor high-quality stainless steel saucepans such as the All-Clad brand. Do not buy aluminum, which is soft, porous, and reactive to certain foods; it can create questionable chemical compounds in your food. It is worth the investment to buy a few good saucepans.

Kitchen Techniques

ALMOND SOAKING: To soak almonds 8 hours or overnight in cool water. Soaking releases enzymes in the nuts and makes them easier to digest, not to mention delicious and versatile.

DESTEM: To remove the stems from large, leafy greens. Hold the stem in one hand and cup the other hand around the bottom of the leaf. Gently squeeze and strip the leaf off the stem with one pull. Chop the leaf for cooking and discard the stem or save it for broth.

DRY ROAST: To roast spices lightly in a dry pan, just until they begin to release their oils and aromas.

GRIND: To slowly break down spices, seeds, and nuts by hand in a mortar and pestle or in an electric grinder (use a coffee grinder that is reserved for spices or a small attachment for your food processor). Most spices in traditional Ayurvedic cookery are freshly ground by hand for each meal.

HAND BLEND: To make a puree (or to churn yogurt with water) by immersing a hand blender in the cooking pot and processing food until smooth. Keep the blender submerged and turn it off before taking it out of the liquid. A tall, wide-mouth canning jar works great for beverages.

QUICK SOAK: To bring water and a grain or legume to a rolling boil for 5 minutes, then cover and let sit for 1 hour. This will have the same effect as soaking overnight.

RINSE: To remove impurities from grains and legumes by rinsing with cool water. Add the dry item to a saucepan and cover with water. Agitate the water with your fingers until it becomes cloudy. Pour the water and grain or legume through a mesh strainer. Rinse under the faucet until the water runs clear.

SOAK: To cut down cooking times by soaking grains and legumes in cool water anywhere from 1 hour (for grains and small beans) to overnight. Rinse the grains or beans well first, put them in a bowl with twice the amount of water, and cover. The longer an item soaks, the faster it will cook. Remember to reduce cooking water in the recipe if you soaked first. Any soak water that remains can be used for cooking.

SPROUT: To soak dried foods such as nuts, seeds, and beans in fresh water to revive them, then rinse daily until they grow tails. Sprouts have very high nutritional value and increase digestive fire. This book makes use of sprouted mung beans and almonds.

STEAM SAUTÉ: To cook in a frying pan, covered, with a small amount of water and no oil.

TEMPER: To fry spices lightly in oil on medium heat until they release essential oils, thereby increasing aroma and flavor and adding "temperance" to the dish. The spices and oil (called "tempering") are often poured into a dal or stew at the end of cooking.

VEGGIE PREP: To dice, slice, or coarsely chop vegetables and store in airtight glass containers for use the next day. Doing your veggie prep on a day off or a slow day is a great way to save time and still be able to cook fresh meals.

APPENDIX 4
TABLE OF FOODS AND MAHA GUNAS

Foods	Sattvic	Rajasic	Tamasic
Fruits	Most fresh, ripe fruit: plums, peaches, apples, pears, grapes, berries, cherries, apricots, figs, bananas, melons, pomegranates, raisins, cranberries	Sour fruits: oranges, lemons (in excess), unripe mango, tamarind, guava Canned fruits Dried dates	Fruits that are frozen, overripe, or out of season
Vegetables	Most fresh, seasonal vegetables: fennel, kale, Swiss chard, summer and winter squashes, cabbage, carrots, sweet potatoes and yams, turnips, parsnips, beets, cucumbers, leafy greens, celery	Olives, garlic, onion, white potatoes, bell pepper, eggplant, tomatoes, chilies, spicy radishes, spicy greens and cruciferous vegetables (in excess), pickles	Mushrooms, pumpkin (in excess) Vegetables that are frozen, GMO, wilted, or out of season
Grains	Rice (brown, red, white basmati), wild rice, quinoa, amaranth, teff, kamut, millet, buckwheat, barley, oats	White flour Dry grains (in excess): corn, millet, buckwheat	Wheat
Beans	Small beans: mung beans, lentils, black beans,* sprouted	Large beans: chickpeas, cannellini, kidney, pinto	Isolated soy protein
Dairy	Nonhomogenized cow's milk, homemade yogurt, goat's milk	Eggs, sour cream, cottage cheese, store-bought/sour yogurt, hard or aged cheeses, cream, ice cream	All cheeses, eggs, processed milk, cold milk, ice cream

Foods	Sattvic	Rajasic	Tamasic
Fats	Ghee, coconut oil and coconut meat Raw nuts and seeds: almonds, cashews, pecans,* walnuts,* sesame seeds, hemp seeds, chia seeds, flaxseeds, sunflower seeds	Pumpkin seeds and avocado (in excess), fried foods	Margarines, canola oil, lard, peanuts, rancid fats (old, or vegetable and nut oils cooked at high heat), roasted nuts, packaged pastries
Spices	Turmeric, cardamom, coriander, cumin, fennel, cinnamon, ginger, hing (asafatida, see the glossary (page 319)	Salt, vinegar, hot sauce, cayenne, black pepper	Monosodium glutamate (MSG)
Extras	Herbal teas: (licorice, fennel, ginger)	Kombucha, coffee, caffeine, fermented foods (unless homemade), bubbly water, alcohol, packaged snack foods	Meat, fish, fried foods, fast foods, leftovers, microwaved foods, drugs and alcohol, potato chips
Sweets	Coconut sugar, maple syrup, raw cane juice, raw honey	White sugar, brown sugar, molasses	White sugar, soft drinks, artificial sweeteners, cooked honey

In moderation (one or two times per week)

GLOSSARY

Sanskrit Terms

ABHYANGA: A warm oil massage using strokes in a specific pattern to support movements of energy according to Ayurvedic principles.

AHAMKARA: The ego; a function of mind responsible for the principle of individuation.

AHARA: The nutritive liquid resulting from food being broken down in the stomach.

AHIMSA: Nonviolence.

AGNI: Fire element.

AMA: Toxicity in the body resulting from undigested food, experiences, and emotions.

AMLA: Sour taste, a combination of fire and earth elements.

ASHTANGA HRDAYAM: An abridged compilation of the Charaka Samhita written by Vagbhata.

BHAGAVAD GITA: Literally "song of the Lord"; India's most famous yoga scripture.

CHARAKA SAMHITA: The most commonly used foundational text on Ayurveda; written in Sanskrit, likely by a group of people at least two thousand years ago.

DINACHARYA: Daily routine.

DOSHA: Literally "that which is at fault"; essential biological compounds present in the body.

GUNA: Strand; quality.

JATHARA AGNI: The digestive fire in the stomach.

INDRIYAS: The senses.

KALA: Time, specifically time of day, year, and life

KAPHA: The energy of structure and lubrication; cohesion.

KASHAYA: Astringent taste, a combination of air and earth elements.

KATU: Pungent taste, a combination of fire and air elements.

KICHARI/KICHADI: A general name for a soupy rice and legume dish; phonetic spelling varies by region.

LAVANA: Salty taste, a combination of fire and water elements.

MADHURA: Sweet taste, a combination of water and earth elements.

NASYA: To administer medicines through the nasal cavity.

RASA: Literally, "sap, juice, or mood"; refers to the classification of taste according to the qualities of a substance, as in *shad rasa*.

OJAS: Literally "vigor"; the cream of the nutrient fluid in the body; the essence of immunity.

PANCHA MAHABHUTAS: The five great elements—space, air, fire, water, and earth.

PITTA: That which transforms or digests.

PRAJNAPARADHA: Literally, "crime against intelligence."

PRANA: Vital energy of the universe.

PRASAD: Food shared by devotees that has first been offered to God.

PRATYAHARA: Withdrawal of the senses.

RAJAS: One of the three gunas, or primary qualities of consciousness; kinetic, dynamic energy; passion.

RASA DHATU: The first of the seven tissue layers; includes white blood cells, lymph fluid, and blood plasma.

RISHIS: The sages of ancient India.

SATTVA: One of the three gunas, or primary qualities of consciousness; the energy of equilibrium; clarity.

SATTVAVAJAYA: Victory over the mind; refers to the body of therapies used to encourage mental balance.

SHAD RASA: Six tastes—sweet, sour, salty, pungent, bitter, astringent—used to classify foods and medicines according to qualities.

SHIRO ABHYANGA: Head/scalp massage with oil.

SUKHA: Happiness; good space.

TAMAS: One of the three gunas, or primary qualities of consciousness; inertia; darkness.

TEJAS: Subtle, metabolic fire.

THALI: A meal consisting of various dishes that includes all six tastes; derives from the word for a round platter used to serve food.

TIKTA: Bitter, a combination of ether and air elements.

VATA: That which moves.

VIPAKA: Postdigestive effect; the effect a substance has on the digestive tract, after being digested in the stomach.

VIRYA: Ultimate potency of a substance; the effect on the body of heating or cooling.

Less Common Ingredients

AJWAIN: *Trachyspermum ammi*, also known as bishop's weed; native to India, the seeds of this plant are used in cooking, and the whole plant is used in Ayurvedic medicine. The seed resembles caraway and tastes similar to anise seed.

BROWN LENTIL: The most commonly found lentil variety; color ranges from khaki to brown; larger than the French lentil; shaped like a flying saucer; good for sprouting.

CORIANDER: The seed of the cilantro plant; round; green or light brown in color.

CURRY LEAVES: Native to India, the dark green leaves of the curry plant, which are commonly used in southern Indian cooking for flavor and aroma. Dried curry leaf loses its aroma; frozen leaves will darken, like basil, but retain their flavor. Do not refrigerate.

CURRY POWDER: A Western invention reflecting a variable mix of spices used in southern Asian cooking; usually includes, but is not limited to, turmeric, chili, coriander, and cumin.

DAL: A soupy Indian dish made from any variety of legumes; originally referred to the legume of the pigeon pea bush, known as *tur dal*. In this book, *dal* generally refers to a mung bean or lentil or the soup made from these legumes, as in "mung dal."

FRENCH LENTIL: Sometimes called Le Puy lentil (only if it was actually grown in the Le Puy region of France); when cultivated in other countries, it is called French or green lentil. These lentils are small and dark green, and they retain their shape when cooked.

HING: Also known as *asafoetida*; a dried gum resin derived from the root of a giant fennel varietal; sold powdered and mixed with flour, or in chunky granules; commonly used in Indian vegetarian cooking to provide a strong, oniony flavor.

MEDJOOL DATE: A soft, moist fruit of the date palm; prized among dates as the largest, sweetest, and most flavorful.

MUNG BEAN: Also known as moong and green gram in India; a small, oval-shaped bean used in both sweet and savory dishes; commonly found in bulk bins; considered lightest and easiest-to-digest legume in Ayurveda.

MUSTARD SEED: Indian cooking uses black mustard seeds, not the yellow ones used to make yellow mustard sauce; small, round seeds; hallmark is its bitter and pungent taste.

RED LENTIL: Orange in color; commonly used in soups and easy to find; actually a brown lentil with the skin removed and the bean split; dissolves completely when cooked for improved digestibility; shorter cook time and less fiber than the brown lentil.

SPLIT MUNG BEANS: Green mung beans that have been hulled and split in half; yellow in color, found at Indian and Asian grocery stores; dissolve completely when cooked; Ayurveda's easiest-to-digest legume.

TAKRA: Fresh buttermilk, produced by removing the fat from whole-milk yogurt through churning and diluting with water; used before meals to digest ama and after meals to improve digestion.

RESOURCES

I am grateful to the following books and their authors, without which this book might not have come into being. These are all excellent resources for further reading.

Agnivesa. *Charaka Samhita*. Translated by Ram Karan Sharma and Vaidya Bhagwan Dash. Varanasi: Chowkhamba Krishnadas Academy, 2015.

Dasa, Satyanarayana. *Bhagavad Gita*. Vrindavan, India: Jiva Institute of Vaishnava Studies, 2014.

Feuerstein, Georg. *The Encyclopedia of Yoga and Tantra*. Boulder, CO: Shambhala, 2011.

Frawley, David. *Ayurveda and the Mind*. Twin Lakes, WI: Lotus Press, 1996.

Freeman, Richard. *Mirror of Yoga*. Boulder, CO: Shambhala, 2012.

Huber, Cheri. *Making a Change for Good*. Boulder, CO: Shambhala, 2007.

Lad, Vasant. *Textbook of Ayurveda: Fundamental Principles*. Albuquerque, NM: Ayurvedic Press, 2002.

Maki, Bhavani Silvia. *The Yogi's Roadmap: The Patanjali Yoga Sutra as a Journey to Self-Realization*. Hanalei, HI: Viveka Press, 2013.

Mitchell, Stephen. *The Bhagavad Gita: A New Translation*. New York: Three Rivers Press, 2000.

Morningstar, Amadea. *Ayurvedic Cooking for Westerners*. Twin Lakes, WI: Lotus Press, 1995.

Svoboda, Robert E. *Prakriti*. Twin Lakes, WI: Lotus Press, 1998.

Vagbhata. *Ashtanga Hrdayam*. 6th ed. Translated by K. R. Srikantha Murthy. Varanasi: Chowkhamba Krishnadas Academy, 2009.

Vidyaranya, Swami. *Panchadasi*. Hollywood, CA: Vedantra Press, 1967.

Welch, Claudia. *How the Art of Science Makes the Science More Effective*. London: Singing Dragon, 2015.

Ayurvedic Suppliers

Banyan Botanicals
Herbs and spices, massage oils, dinacharya supplies
www.banyanbotanicals.com

Pure Indian Foods
Pure ghee
www.pureindianfoods.com

Sarada Ayurvedic Remedies
Handmade body and beauty products, massage oils
www.saradausa.com

Starwest Botanicals
Best asafetida powder (hing)
www.starwestbotanicals.com

ACKNOWLEDGMENTS

My most sincere thanks to all those who helped make this book happen in a variety of ways. Notably:

My family: Mom, Dad, and brother O'Donnell, who continue to eat my recipes, and Rich Ray, for listening.

The editors: Juree Sondker, Dr. Robert Svoboda, Erin Casperson (extra thanks), Hilary Garivaltis, Dr. Anusha Seghal; and Rochelle Bourgeault, who started it all.

Designer Allison Meierding, who has a wonderful eye.

Cara Brostrom, who contributes a lot more than photography.

Head recipe tester Carabeth Connolly.

The recipe testing team: Christie Rosen, Rochelle Bourgault, Shawna Boles, Julia Featheringill, Mercedes Von Deck, Betsy Bowden, Rebecca Davis, Zuzana Angelovicova, Pallavi Nagesha, Lisa Matthews, Renee Egan, Valerie Lauro, Jessica Babine, and Amy Thornton.

Cooking superstars Risa Horn and Carabeth Connolly.

Kitchen photoshoot location: Bruce and Marcia Humphrey and Sarah Rowe.

Writing locations: Vaidygrama, Frank Smith, Linda Borman, and Laura Cashel.

All the folks at Shambhala Publications.

Boston Ayurveda School faculty and students.

Special thanks from Cara Brostrom:

My family: Chris Okerberg and my daughters.

The memory of Echo Trobridge, for all of the help and support she gave me and my family during the making of this book. And also for the beautiful handmade pottery featured in these pages.

Adrienne Wilson also for looking after Evelyn.

Extra thanks to Rochelle Bourgault and Allison Meierding.

My sister, Renee, for all of her delicious and inspiring gluten-free baked goodies. And my mom for always cheering me on.

INDEX

ABOUT US

CARA BROSTROM

Kate O'Donnell is a nationally certified Ayurvedic practitioner, Ashtanga yoga teacher, and author of *The Everyday Ayurveda Cookbook: A Seasonal Guide to Eating and Living Well.* She has made twenty extended trips to India and continues to travel there annually for study. She also teaches Ayurveda internationally.

At age nineteen, Kate went to India for a semester abroad to teach English and study environmental science. She took a semester off from school to stay, practice yoga, and travel to as many parts of India as she could in six months. During that time, she ate an indigestible amount of unfamiliar foods and ended up at an Ayurvedic doctor's office. Profound experiences of Ashtanga yoga and Ayurveda, as well as an avid interest in the healing powers of food, have inspired her study and practice of the ancient arts for the past twenty years. Kate is the director of an Ashtanga yoga program in Boston, codirector of the Boston Ayurveda School, and a contributor to many publications. She teaches courses, cooking classes, seasonal cleanses, and lifestyle retreats when she isn't practicing yoga or having a chai.

WWW.KATEODONNELL.YOGA // @KATEODONNELL.AYURVEDA

HANNAH GUNNELL

Cara Brostrom is a lifestyle, editorial, and fine art photographer. As a visual storyteller, her photography documents the landscapes, objects, and moments that reveal our modern lives.

After years of traveling, Cara put down roots in Boston, where she met Kate O'Donnell and nurtured an ardent interest in yoga and Ayurveda. Through the camera lens, Cara specializes in photographing the subtle energy of yoga and the beauty of natural and wholesome foods. In addition to the inspired food and lifestyle photography within these pages, she brings to this book her recipe development expertise in adapting traditional Ayurvedic dishes to the Western palate.

Her photography and writing have been exhibited and published in the United States, Canada, Scandinavia, and the United Kingdom. She lives in Massachusetts with her family.

WWW.CARABROSTROM.COM // @CARABROS